ORCA **Think**

*Question, connect and take action to become better citizens
with a brighter future. Now that's smart thinking!*

IN IT TO WIN IT

SPORTS AND THE CLIMATE CRISIS

ERIN SILVER

ILLUSTRATED BY
PUI YAN FONG

ORCA BOOK PUBLISHERS

Published in Canada and the United States in 2024 by Orca Book Publishers.
orcabook.com

Library and Archives Canada Cataloguing in Publication
Title: In it to win it : sports and the climate crisis / Erin Silver ; illustrated by Pui Yan Fong.
Names: Silver, Erin, 1980- author. | Fong, Pui Yan, illustrator.
Series: Orca think ; 15.
Description: Series statement: Orca think ; 15 | Includes bibliographical references and index.
Identifiers: Canadiana (print) 20230485308 | Canadiana (ebook) 20230485324 |
ISBN 9781459837263 (hardcover) | ISBN 9781459837270 (PDF) | ISBN 9781459837287 (EPUB)
Subjects: LCSH: Sports—Environmental aspects—Juvenile literature. |
LCSH: Sports—Social aspects—Juvenile literature. |
LCSH: Climatic changes—Social aspects—Juvenile literature. |
LCSH: Sustainability—Social aspects—Juvenile literature.
Classification: LCC GV706.5 .S55 2024 | DDC j306.4/83—dc23

Library of Congress Control Number: 2023941261

Summary: Part of the nonfiction Orca Think series for middle-grade readers, this illustrated book examines how sports are affecting the planet, what climate change means for athletes and sporting events, and what young people can do to make sports sustainable for the future.

Orca Book Publishers is committed to reducing the consumption of nonrenewable resources in the production of our books. We make every effort to use materials that support a sustainable future.

Orca Book Publishers gratefully acknowledges the support for its publishing programs provided by the following agencies: the Government of Canada, the Canada Council for the Arts and the Province of British Columbia through the BC Arts Council and the Book Publishing Tax Credit.

Cover and interior artwork by Pui Yan Fong
Design by Troy Cunningham
Edited by Kirstie Hudson

Printed and bound in South Korea.

27   26   25   24   •   1   2   3   4

*To my two
amazing athletes.
I will always be your
biggest fan.*

CONTENTS

A CLIMATE COMEBACK IS UNDERWAY

I recently volunteered to help a baseball team with a garbage cleanup in my hometown of Toronto. The tight-knit group of 12-year-olds was on a mission to tidy up their ballpark. Led by a grass-roots organization called Don't Mess with the Don, the young players were appalled by the number of rusty bicycle wheels, rotting baseballs and discarded food wrappers that filled their garbage bags. By the end of the day, the team was exhausted but also exhilarated—they had made a difference for the planet and for all the other players who use the park regularly.

The North York Blues baseball team cleans up their home field in Toronto. They were surprised at how much garbage they were able to collect in one day.

ERIN SILVER

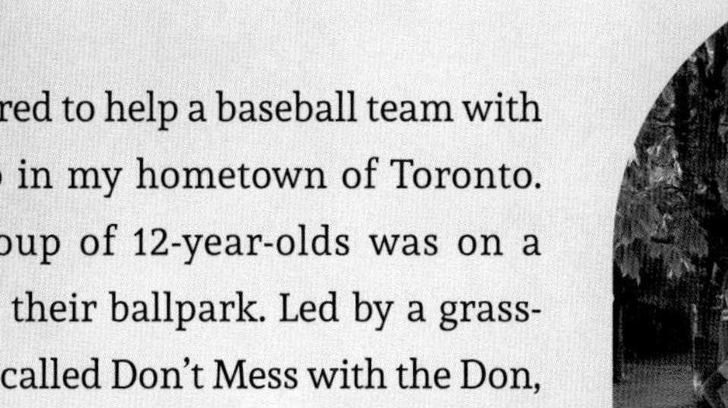

1

As leaders and influencers, athletes—and fans too—can play a big role in raising awareness, taking action and spurring change when it comes to the planet. The fact is, our climate is warming up—and fast. It's not called **climate change** anymore—it's a **climate crisis**. Sports aren't solely to blame for **global warming**, but they contribute to the worldwide problem.

And while it's easy to get down—as if the opposing team is winning 10–0 in a championship baseball game—there is hope. Many encouraging changes are underway, and kids are part of this *climate comeback.* They're recycling tennis balls, using sustainable transportation to get to practices and games, and speaking up about the changes needed to ensure that they can keep playing their favorite sports in the years ahead. Whether you're a future professional athlete or a sports fan who loves being on the sidelines, you have a lot of power to effect change. Now go on and play for the planet!

CHAPTER ONE

SPORTS VERSUS THE PLANET

When you're playing soccer or watching a professional baseball game on TV, the last thing you're thinking about is how that sport is affecting the planet. You're having fun with your friends, cheering on your favorite players or thinking about what snack to eat next. And that's great. Sports should be fun. They are games, after all! Sports unite billions of people—they form one of the biggest industries on the planet. But sports come at a cost to the planet. Building arenas, traveling to games, watering fields and wearing your favorite jerseys all contribute to the climate crisis.

KEEPING SCORE

Experts have tried to calculate just how much activities like soccer and football heat up the planet. They look at the *carbon dioxide (CO$_2$) emissions* athletics add to the environment. A report called *Playing Against the Clock* found that

Even lighting a stadium uses a lot of energy—and not all of it comes from clean sources.
FSTOP123/GETTY IMAGES

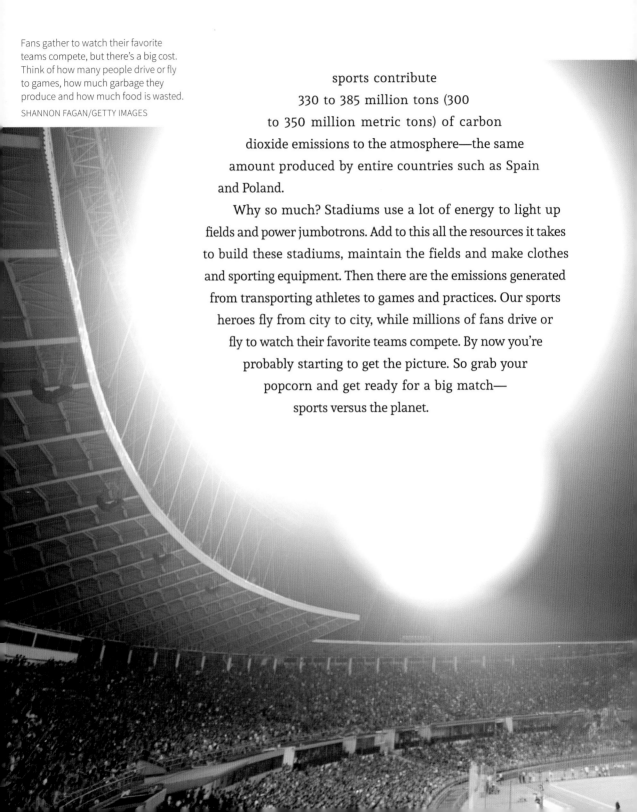

Fans gather to watch their favorite teams compete, but there's a big cost. Think of how many people drive or fly to games, how much garbage they produce and how much food is wasted.
SHANNON FAGAN/GETTY IMAGES

sports contribute 330 to 385 million tons (300 to 350 million metric tons) of carbon dioxide emissions to the atmosphere—the same amount produced by entire countries such as Spain and Poland.

Why so much? Stadiums use a lot of energy to light up fields and power jumbotrons. Add to this all the resources it takes to build these stadiums, maintain the fields and make clothes and sporting equipment. Then there are the emissions generated from transporting athletes to games and practices. Our sports heroes fly from city to city, while millions of fans drive or fly to watch their favorite teams compete. By now you're probably starting to get the picture. So grab your popcorn and get ready for a big match— sports versus the planet.

TRANSPORTATION

AIR TRAVEL

Of all the CO_2 emissions produced by the sports industry, transportation is responsible for the most. Think about it. If you had to travel across the world to compete in the Olympics, how would you get there? You would most likely fly. The math is complicated— even Einstein would have a hard time calculating it. Here's how you might try:

The number of Olympic athletes, coaches and support staff plus family and friends plus fans plus tourists multiplied by the number of miles each person had to fly or drive to get to the Olympics equals the amount of carbon emissions in metric tons.

Erin Silver

Since 1,000 miles (1,600 kilometers) of air travel creates approximately 500 pounds (226 kilograms) of carbon emissions per passenger, it's safe to say that getting people to international sporting events puts a lot of emissions into the atmosphere—emissions that stay there for centuries and contribute to global warming. Here are a few statistics we do know:

Five million fans came to watch the FIFA World Cup in Russia in 2018. All that travel produced about 1.7 million tons (1.6 million metric tons) of carbon dioxide. That's the same amount produced by providing electricity to 500,000 homes a year.

The National Basketball Association (NBA) flew staff and athletes more than 1.3 million miles (2 million kilometers) during the 2018–2019 season before the pandemic grounded all flights.

With 3,000 athletes competing and 150,000 fans invited to attend, the Beijing Winter Games produced the equivalent of 1.4 million tons (1.3 million metric tons) of carbon dioxide, the same amount generated by 220,000 cars in a year.

Traveling to international competitions, such as the Olympic Games and professional soccer matches, is a major source of emissions.

BAONA/GETTY IMAGES

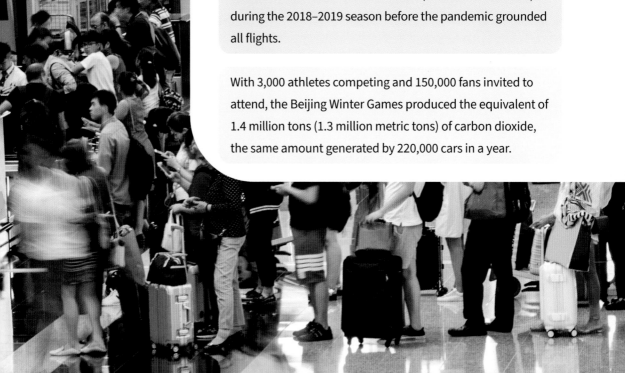

ADVICE FROM A PRO

DR. SETH WYNES

Seth Wynes is an expert on climate solutions at Concordia University in Montreal. He looks at environmental problems and how ordinary people can be part of the solution. One area he's focusing on now is sports, especially how professional athletes in the major leagues—the National Football League (NFL), National Hockey League (NHL), Major League Baseball (MLB) and National Basketball Association (NBA)—get to games. He compared data from 2018 (before the pandemic) to 2020 (during the peak) and found some surprising results.

"The NFL has the most emissions per game—almost double what the other big leagues produce," Wynes says. "Even though they have fewer games in a season, they fly straight home after every one." But there's good news. Wynes found that small changes to how games are scheduled can have a significant effect. "To reduce the impact from air travel, it would be better for leagues to play multiple games in the same location before moving on."

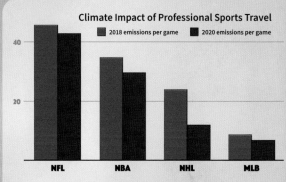

Climate Impact of Professional Sports Travel

■ 2018 emissions per game ■ 2020 emissions per game

Emissions measured in metric tons of carbon dioxide

Source: Seth Wynes

He says MLB is an example of a league that already does this. Teams play a series of games in one city before moving to the next. Hockey isn't organized as well. "In hockey, the Boston Bruins might come to Toronto for one game and fly to their next game in Vancouver and then back to Toronto later in the season for another game."

During the pandemic, teams made several changes, including staying in one place for more games and playing them back to back, so players wouldn't get sick. "If you do this in a normal season, the big leagues could save 22 percent of all air-travel emissions."

Wynes says it's important for leagues to act now. Every metric ton of emissions we cut matters, and we need to reduce as many metric tons as quickly as possible. "We don't want so much wildfire smoke that kids can't play outside in the summer," he says. "We don't want it to get so hot we can't go ice skating in winter."

CARS

Another problem is the emissions released by cars. That's because most amateur athletes travel by car to and from practices and games. Some teams travel every day of the week. Car emissions contribute harmful pollutants such as carbon monoxide and carbon dioxide into the atmosphere. And there's a big NFL pre-game tradition that's a problem. It's called **tailgating**. Fans **idle** their cars as they slowly make their way into parking lots for a party hours before kickoff and then use charcoal grills to barbecue food. One study looked at levels of pollution before and after football games at North Carolina's Carter-Finley Stadium.

Researchers found that starting 6 hours before games, pollution levels were 20 times higher than what's considered moderate air quality. Sometimes air pollution didn't go back to low levels until 12 hours after a game.

HOW AUTO RACING IS GETTING GREENER

Car racing is a sport that literally runs on gas. And that's a problem for eco-conscious racers like Lewis Hamilton. As much as the world-champion driver loves racing, he doesn't understand why the sport isn't promising to become *carbon-neutral* until 2030. "The world is slow to change, and I don't see it changing drastically anytime soon," he says.

Recently Formula 1 (F1) added up its total carbon emissions. Not including the way fans get to races, F1's emissions clocked in at 282,800 tons (256,551 metric tons). Here's a breakdown for the season:

HIT OR MISS?

The Beijing Winter Olympics in 2022 claimed to be the first carbon-neutral Games. Organizers planted over 197,000 acres (80,000 hectares) of forest, used new low-impact climate technology to cool ice rinks, shuttled people around in fuel-efficient vehicles and powered events with wind and solar energy. To cut its footprint, organizers bought 1.7 million **carbon credits**, each of which is supposed to neutralize a metric ton of carbon dioxide emissions. But some experts say their efforts were more **greenwashing** than green and that the Beijing Olympics didn't actually help the climate crisis.

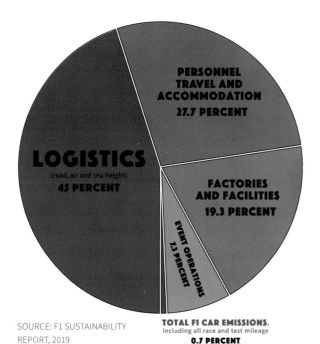

LOGISTICS
(road, air and sea freight)
45 PERCENT

PERSONNEL TRAVEL AND ACCOMMODATION
27.7 PERCENT

FACTORIES AND FACILITIES
19.3 PERCENT

EVENT OPERATIONS
7.3 PERCENT

TOTAL F1 CAR EMISSIONS,
including all race and test mileage
0.7 PERCENT

SOURCE: F1 SUSTAINABILITY REPORT, 2019

Formula 1 race-car driver Lewis Hamilton cares about the planet. He thinks racing can become greener faster.
GOVERNO DO ESTADO DE SÃO PAULO/ WIKIMEDIA COMMONS/CC BY 2.0

Car racing is going electric, which is good news for the planet! Fast new electric cars show that it's possible to have more environmentally friendly races.

FORMULA E

To help with this problem, F1 plans to have more sustainable races by 2025. Meanwhile, the National Association for Stock Car Auto Racing, better known as NASCAR, uses fuel that reduces **greenhouse gas** emissions by 20 percent and increases a car's horsepower. A **biofuel** blended with ethanol, it's made with wheat, corn and gasoline. To offset its emissions, NASCAR has planted more than 500,000 trees across the United States in areas hit by natural disasters like hurricanes, which can be caused by climate change. Fans can buy trees online if they want to help.

Recently auto racing launched Formula E (E for *electric*). Founded by Alejandro Agag and Jean Todt, Formula E racers compete in fully electric cars. The racing series is so eco-conscious that it serves low-carbon meals at events, made with vegetables or with chicken, which has a smaller footprint than beef. Automakers, including Audi, BMW, Jaguar, Mercedes, Nissan and Porsche, have all committed to Formula E. Keep an eye out for Extreme E, a new racing series that will see

SCORE!
PROFESSIONAL SPORTS ORGANIZATIONS ARE STEPPING UP

Many European football (soccer) teams partnered with several cities to offer free public transportation passes to fans so they could travel around FIFA host cities on game day for free.

The French Table Tennis Federation announced that at least 80 percent of its teams' travel will be by public transportation or car sharing.

From 2030 on, all Olympic Games must be carbon-neutral (have no impact on the planet). The International Olympic Committee wants to go a step further and make all Olympic Games *climate-positive*.

all-electric SUVs compete in areas around the world that have been damaged by climate change, such as the Greenland ice cap, to draw attention to the environment.

SPORTS GEAR

CLOTHING

Hockey might be Canada's national pastime, but young fans are wondering how much jerseys and equipment are affecting the planet, and asking whether we can do better. A group of students at Queen's University in Kingston, Ontario, wrote a paper asking whether it was necessary for all NHL teams to have three versions of their jerseys for one hour of play. Meanwhile, in football (called soccer in North America) it's common for professional clubs to provide new kits (jerseys) for every player every game. Plus, new team sponsorships mean uniforms are used and replaced at least once a season.

When you're done using your sports uniforms and equipment, what do you do with them? One great idea is to give them to kids who can use them.
PETER MULLER/GETTY IMAGES

Many students, athletes and organizations are concerned about the amount of resources, like water and energy, that are needed to produce the jerseys, many of which are made of synthetic fabrics such as polyester and spandex, which are derived from **petroleum.** When they're washed, these fabrics release **microplastics**, or tiny pieces of plastic, that eventually find their way from our water systems to oceans and other bodies of water. And when they're thrown away, they can take 200 years to decompose in a landfill. A lot of the time, however, unwanted or unused clothes are burned, producing a high amount of carbon dioxide. None of this is good for marine life or the air.

While some teams are starting to use recycled fabrics, the problem is bigger than just the NHL and football (soccer).

HIT OR MISS?

In Australia and New Zealand alone, more than 1,100 tons (1,000 metric tons) of basketballs, tennis balls, rackets, and ski boards, boots and poles end up in the landfill each year. The Australian government recently launched a new program to collect and recycle as much used sporting equipment as possible. Many other countries and organizations are also trying to keep used sporting equipment out of the landfill. Ask your parents to help you check out sites like SidelineSwap or Facebook Marketplace to sell your used equipment. Or donate it to kids who can use it.

When you add in jerseys from other professional teams, plus college and amateur sports, it could double or triple this problem. You might even have several years' worth of old jerseys in your closet.

EQUIPMENT

Then there's the issue with equipment. Of course, helmets, chest protectors and cleats are necessary for safety. But they're all made of plastic and foam and can't be recycled. What happens to all that gear when players grow out of it? The majority of our shin guards, knee pads and chest protectors get thrown in the garbage. It can take 1,000 years for things like protective gear and cleats to decompose.

There are a few ways to lessen the impact of sports gear on the planet. For instance, researchers are experimenting with using cork instead of foam in things like helmets. Cork is a natural material that comes from trees, and tests show it may be just as effective as synthetic foam at preventing head injuries. Other organizations, from secondhand stores to local teams, are encouraging people to swap or donate gently used equipment so it can be put to good use rather than landing in the trash. And there are even more initiatives underway.

TAKING ACTION

The way we make and throw away sports clothing, shoes and equipment is a problem, but some sports companies are changing the way things are done.

California-based activewear company Vuori makes its gear with things like recycled plastic bottles, certified organic cotton and nylon fishing-net waste. It's also cutting plastic packaging, offsetting its emissions and working with the community to organize beach cleanups.

Nike Grind partners with different companies to grind up and recycle old shoes and fabric scraps to make everything from football fields to furniture. About 130 million pounds (59 million kilograms) of Nike Grind materials have been recycled into other products since the program began in 1992.

UK-based sporting goods store Decathlon fixes repairable products so people can use them longer rather than throw them out. And its Second Life program lets others buy those repaired products like bikes, rackets and skis at discounted prices to give others a chance to try out a new sport.

As the official ball provider for the NFL, US Open and NBA, Wilson Sporting Goods is setting an example by using more sustainable materials and less packaging and plastic. The company also collects and recycles tennis balls (20 million in three years) and has planted a million trees to offset its footprint.

FOOD WASTE AND GARBAGE

All those nachos, hot dogs and single-use plastic soda bottles you buy at the stadium aren't good for the health of the planet. Then there's the food waste. In 2021 during the Olympic Games in Tokyo, 175 tons (158 metric tons) of food went untouched by athletes. That was in addition to

the 300,000 bento boxes made for staff and volunteers that also went to waste. Big sporting venues use a lot of gas, electricity and water to cook food for thousands of people at once—all to produce food that could end up in the trash. But things are starting to change.

Chef T gave my son a behind-the-scenes tour of the food operations at Oracle Park—and they got to make pizza!
ERIN SILVER

IN THE SPOTLIGHT
ORACLE PARK

My son and I took a trip to one of the most sustainable stadiums in the United States—Oracle Park, home of the San Francisco Giants baseball team—to learn more about its green efforts. We went behind the scenes with the ballpark's head chef, known as Chef T. He told us all about the things he and his team are doing to leave a positive mark on the planet. They grow fresh foods in a garden behind center field, from artichokes and blueberries to kumquats and thyme, which are used at concession stands throughout the Giants' ballpark. The stadium also uses energy-efficient appliances and fryers that cut the amount of gas needed by 32 percent and reduce the amount of cooking oil needed by 12 percent. In all, these efforts save enough energy to fry another

BUILDING, MAINTAINING AND OPERATING SPORTS VENUES

STADIUMS

All sports facilities, from new stadiums for the Olympic Games to your local ski hill, have a carbon footprint. That's because it takes a lot of concrete to build new facilities. Concrete is the most widely used substance in the world after water. But the cement industry is also one of the main producers of carbon dioxide, after coal, oil and gas. Producing concrete creates

110 tons (99 metric tons) of their famous garlic fries. At the end of every Giants game, they donate left-over food to local organizations, and staff separate garbage, recyclables and food waste into piles in a huge (and smelly!) facility to divert as much waste as possible from land-fills. Staff help keep about 98 percent of waste out of the landfill. In the future Oracle Park will be even more sustainable through strategies like banning plastic bottles entirely.

Oracle Park is using more efficient cooking equipment and reducing wasteful practices in its concession stands—including at the famous Gilroy Garlic Fries stand.
ERIN SILVER

Have you ever thought about how much water it takes to maintain a golf course?

PETER ADAMS/GETTY IMAGES

4 to 8 percent of the world's carbon dioxide emissions each year. So much is used in building projects that by the time you finish reading this sentence, the world's construction industry will have poured more than 19,000 bathtubs of the gray stuff.

FACILITIES

Maintaining large swaths of grass, from golf courses to baseball diamonds, requires a lot of water. Depending on its location, an 18-hole golf course can use about 2 billion gallons (7.5 billion liters) of water per day. Even in the parched state of Utah, about 38 million gallons (144 million liters) of water is used daily on golf courses—enough to fill almost 58 Olympic-sized swimming pools. That's a lot of water at a time when some states are facing **megadrought**. On top of that, poisonous **pesticides** are often used to keep the bugs away.

Creating snow for the 2022 Winter Olympics in Beijing— a city plagued by drought—was a big deal. Making those fake flakes used 49 million gallons of water (186 million liters)— a million bathtubs' worth. When you take water from a place that already doesn't have enough, it can affect the food supply, leave the soil vulnerable to **erosion** and make it hard for people to access water when they need it.

Maintaining the ice at hockey arenas is a problem too. Most NHL ice rinks use refrigerants called ***hydrochlorofluorocarbons (HCFCs)*** or ***hydrofluorocarbons (HFCs)*** to keep the ice

from melting. These artificial chemical compounds destroy the earth's **ozone layer**, which acts like an umbrella to protect us from the sun's harmful UV-B rays. These chemicals also trap heat, making the earth's temperature rise. In fact, coolants like these contribute 11.5 percent of the greenhouse gases in the atmosphere.

MOVING TOWARD CHANGE

Of course, building stadiums, creating artificial snow, freezing ice rinks and watering grass aren't activities that are going to stop. But new standards are making them more sustainable. Many venues and teams are jumping on board to make a difference. We'll look at some of these efforts in the chapters ahead.

WHAT'S THE RUSH?

Climate activists around the world are calling on the sports industry to take action now. Many organizations have signed on to a United Nations pact to become carbon-neutral by 2050. This means that the industry has to cut its emissions—and fast. Global warming is having an adverse impact on athletes—not just on how they perform but whether they can play at all.

SCORE!

Some sports are better for the planet than others:

- RUNNING
- CYCLING
- OPEN-WATER SWIMMING
- SURFING
- AMATEUR SOCCER

Some sports are worse for the planet than others:

- GOLF
- AUTO RACING
- ANY SPORTS THAT USE MOTORIZED BOATS
- SKIING AND SNOWBOARDING
- PROFESSIONAL SPORTS PLAYED IN BIG ARENAS

Many organizations are looking at the impact of sports on the planet in new ways. They want to do their part and lead by example.
ALEX_SCHMIDT/GETTY IMAGES

CHAPTER TWO

A FIERCE OPPONENT

Viewers watched in shock as Russian tennis player Daniil Medvedev swayed on the court. Dizzy and exhausted from Tokyo's suffocating heat and humidity, he hunched over, propping himself up on his knees. Tennis shirt drenched in sweat, he gasped for breath in sauna-like conditions. A medic rushed to the athlete's side, but it was no use. He couldn't catch his breath, and at times he couldn't see. "I will finish the match, but I can die," Medvedev told the chair umpire. After a cold shower to cool his body, Medvedev was able to play.

THE HEAT IS ON

Medvedev's story was scary, and unfortunately he was just one of many athletes during the Tokyo Olympics in 2021 to suffer from the heat. Jessica Judd from the United Kingdom and Lucia Rodriguez of Spain collapsed after their Olympic 10,000-meter races in Tokyo. The temperature during the

It's hard to compete at your best when it's hot and humid outside. Those conditions can make athletes sick.
WESTEND61/GETTY IMAGES

Sports organizers are becoming more aware of factors that make it unsafe for athletes to compete outdoors on certain days.
COROIMAGE/GETTY IMAGES

MARC BRUXELLE/GETTY IMAGES

races was over 100°F (37.8°C) and humidity was at 80 percent. Paula Badosa, a tennis player from Spain, overheated and was pushed off the court in a wheelchair. Her opponent, Czech player Marketa Vondrousova, found a way to beat the heat. She used ice towels to lower her body temperature. The brutal conditions led the International Olympic Committee to shift matches to cooler venues and later times, but the heat still made it hard for athletes to perform their best. Even Tokyo residents were advised to stay indoors—it was hard even for average citizens to breathe.

TOO HOT TO HANDLE

Changes caused by global warming earned the Tokyo Olympics the title for the hottest and most dangerous on record. Future Olympics might not be much better off. Paris, host of the 2024 Summer Games, has faced deadly heat waves in recent years. Los Angeles, which won the bid for the 2028 Games, will host in what has become the peak of wildfire season. Experts say that if we don't do more to protect the planet, only 33 of 645 major cities in the northern hemisphere will be able to host the Games in a climate safe for athletes by 2085. Temperatures have climbed so much that even the Winter Olympic Games are affected by warmer weather and lack of snow.

HIT OR MISS?

Tokyo is cooler and drier in October, which was when the city first hosted the Summer Olympics in 1964. The 1968 Mexico City Olympics were also held in October, when temperatures were more comfortable. But for the last three decades, the Games have taken place in the hottest months, July and August. That's in part because TV networks say summer is the best time to attract the most viewers. Plus they don't compete with fall programming, like professional football, baseball and soccer seasons in North America and Europe. If this scheduling continues, summer competitions are more likely to be played on days where temperatures reach 104 to 113°F (40 to 45°C). How will TV stations fill the airwaves if athletes can't play?

SEEING RED

If you like outdoor activities like cycling or hiking, you might think global warming sounds great. Spring will start earlier, and winters will be shorter. In other words, you'll get more time to enjoy the great outdoors. But global warming doesn't just mean

Cities across the world are seeing hotter temperatures every year, making it dangerous to play outside. This map shows the increase in average summer temperatures in certain areas of the United States since 1970.

MAP COURTESY OF RCC-ACIS

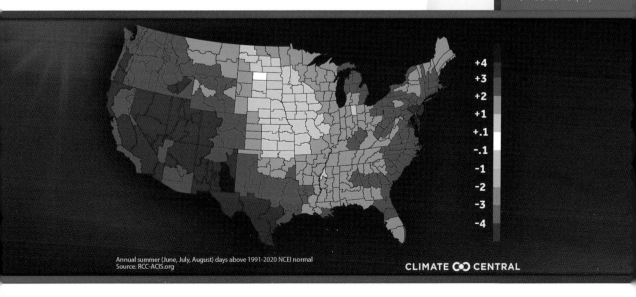

SUMMER WARMING
since 1970 (°F)

+4
+3
+2
+1
+.1
-.1
-1
-2
-3
-4

Annual summer (June, July, August) days above 1991-2020 NCEI normal
Source: RCC-ACIS.org

CLIMATE CO CENTRAL

warmer temperatures. It means that weather patterns all over the world are changing, making some areas really dry while others experience more severe weather, like flooding, storms and scorching temperatures. All these changes may compromise people's ability to play outdoors. It even means that exercising outside could make athletes sick—or worse.

RECOGNIZING THE WARNING SIGNS

Do you know how to tell if the heat is making you sick? Arizona State University's Urban Climate Research Center shows students and coaches when enough is enough. Other research centers are also doing everything they can to educate people on the dangers of heatstroke. The Korey Stringer Institute, established in 2010 at the University of Connecticut, was founded in honor of the NFL offensive lineman who died of exertion-related heat stroke in 2001. The institute's mission is to make sure everyone, from athletes to outdoor workers to military personnel, understands the signs of heat stroke and how to cope.

HIT OR MISS?

The United States National Park Service did a study of the relationship between air temperature and park visitations. They think park attendance could increase 8 to 23 percent by 2060, as their research showed that the number of visitors increased when temperatures were warmer. You might enjoy hiking on a nice day, except that global warming also means weather that is more severe and unpredictable. It's hard to hike on trails washed away by floods. And if drought-stricken forests are burned during a wildfire, you won't be needing your hiking boots for quite a while.

WEATHERING MORE STORMS

Heat isn't the only way climate change affects athletes. Bad weather can stop games before they start. Take football (soccer) as an example. This sport contributes more than 30 million tons (27 million metric tons) of carbon dioxide every year—the same as the

THE SCIENCE OF SWEAT

Heat scientist Matthew Cramer is an expert on how humans are affected by hot temperatures. He spends his days working at Canada's Department of National Defence, researching how service members can work and exercise safely under different conditions. "The frequency, duration and intensity of heat waves are all going up," says Cramer. "This means that more of us will have more encounters with hot weather."
For people in areas where it's already hot, like Texas, Florida and Arizona, for example, it's only going to get worse. "But it's also bad for people in more moderate climates because they're not used to it. They might not know what to do," he says.

He says kids will fare better, though, because they're good at managing their bodies. "They will slow down or stop doing their activity if they don't feel well," says Cramer. "It's not the same for competitive athletes, who are highly motivated to keep going and keep pushing even if they're sick. They ignore the warning signs."

It all comes down to your body's ability to sweat. When you're running really hard, your body sweats to cool itself off. The hotter you get, the more you sweat. When it's too humid, however, that sweat can't evaporate from your skin, making your internal body temperature even higher. That's when you can start to feel dizzy, tired and weak. In some cases, athletes need medical attention. Other times, they can even die. It's important to be aware of how much the climate can affect your health. Cramer offers a few tips:

- Don't exercise outside when it's really hot. Practice or play in the morning or evening, when the sun is lower and temperatures are cooler. Cancel games if it's too hot.
- Drink plenty of water. If you're drinking according to your level of thirst, you'll know you're properly hydrated. (Check out the pee-color test to know if you're getting enough to drink.)
- Avoid the sun, but when you're out in it, wear loose-fitting clothing to give your body a chance to cool off. Wear sunscreen to prevent sunburn and a hat to help shield your eyes.
- Cool off. Keep ice towels in a cooler. During breaks, wrap a cold towel around your neck.
- When training hard or competing in hot weather, coaches or event organizers should keep a tub of water nearby. If someone collapses from the heat, immerse them in the water up to the neck to cool them down and then call for help.

WHAT COLOR IS YOUR URINE?

HYDRATED   DEHYDRATED

"Dark yellow urine is more concentrated, indicating that the body is trying to conserve water because it isn't getting enough."
—Stavros Kavouras

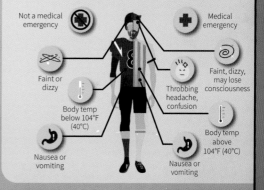

KNOW THE WARNING SIGNS

Exertional heat exhaustion   Exertional heatstroke

Not a medical emergency   Medical emergency

Faint or dizzy

Body temp below 104°F (40°C)

Nausea or vomiting

Throbbing headache, confusion

Faint, dizzy, may lose consciousness

Body temp above 104°F (40°C)

Nausea or vomiting

COURTESY OF ASU

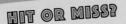

HIT OR MISS?

Do you like fishing? A warmer day might draw you outside to try your luck with your lure. But warmer weather means warmer water—and fewer fish. They head for cooler temperatures, just like humans head for air-conditioned spaces. When fish leave their natural habitat, it sets off a chain reaction, and whole ecosystems begin to change.

entire country of Denmark. If global warming continues, 25 percent of British football fields may be flooded every season for the next 30 years. Bad weather already costs amateur athletes a month of soccer games in the United Kingdom. But increases in storms and flooding from global warming cost every athlete, from Little Leaguers to professionals, valuable playing time.

MARK DADSWELL/GETTY IMAGES

IN THE SPOTLIGHT
AMY STEEL

Australian netball star Amy Steel turned pro at age 15. "Sports were a big passion of mine," says Steel. "I was always playing something—cross-country skiing, basketball, tennis, running, swimming." Her life revolved around sports, and netball (a game like basketball but without backboards or dribbling) was her livelihood—until one stifling hot day changed Steel's life. "Early March in Australia is the end of summer," she explains. "It's when we get most of our 40°C [104°F] days. We had a game two hours away from Melbourne at a stadium that wasn't new. The air wasn't circulating, and we were playing indoors without air-conditioning."

Steel felt overheated before they'd even run, and she'd never experienced such humidity before. Without a breeze or air circulation to help moisture evaporate from her skin, the heat started to build. As the game went on, conditions became riskier and riskier. She played her hardest, despite the conditions. Then, after the game, Steel collapsed. She had no idea that the extreme heat

This minor-league baseball stadium in Iowa flooded in 2019. Changing weather patterns make flooding a bigger problem than it used to be.

would make that game her very last. "I thought I'd be okay," she says. "It didn't feel like a life-changing event at the time. I thought I'd be fine the next day." After seeing doctors and spending months in bed, feeling too dizzy to get up, Steel discovered that she'd had heatstroke and suffered permanent damage from the condition. "I've never been able to play sports again since that day," she says. "There was no way to get better." She was just 26 at the time.

It was ironic. Steel had always worried about the planet, and now global warming had changed her life. With a business degree, she decided to channel her energy into helping some of the world's biggest emitters reduce their carbon footprint. Today she works as a climate-risk manager. "I tell companies and governments what happens if they don't reduce their carbon emissions and show them what that looks like," she explains. "I also teach them how to *decarbonize*. I motivate them to invest more money and to do it quicker." Steel is also a climate-change ambassador. She hopes to make a difference by speaking out and inspiring others to act. "At the end of the day, there are only two things I can do—worry or do something about it," she says. "I'll never have to wonder if I could have taken more action."

> "THERE ARE LOTS OF LITTLE SIMPLE STEPS WE CAN TAKE TO MAKE OUR FOOTPRINT SMALLER."
>
> —Amy Steel, activist and former athlete

This "lightning" bus in Florida keeps students safe during storms. When the lightning horn sounds, students get on the bus and are driven to safety.

ERIN SILVER

WHEN LIGHTNING STRIKES

I was recently in Bradenton, Florida, visiting my son at school when I heard a loud foghorn sounding throughout the campus. Special "lightning" buses pulled up to shuttle students to safety indoors. I didn't know what the horns meant, but weather-safety alerts are nothing new in Florida, known as the lightning capital of the United States. Florida gets 1.2 million lightning strikes every year. Experts say that number is expected to climb by 10 percent for every 1.8°F (1°C) the planet warms. It's a big problem—and not just because student athletes like my son will be stuck indoors more often. Lightning is also hotter than the surface of the sun—it can be 50,000°F (27,760°C). When it strikes, it can set buildings and whole forests on fire. Before anyone can get a wildfire under control, entire swaths of land—homes for humans and animals—can be burned to a crisp. While not all wildfires are caused by lightning, global warming has created perfect conditions for fires to spread, no matter how they were started.

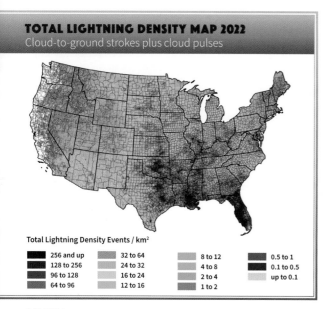

TOTAL LIGHTNING DENSITY MAP 2022
Cloud-to-ground strokes plus cloud pulses

Total Lightning Density Events / km²

256 and up	32 to 64	8 to 12	0.5 to 1
128 to 256	24 to 32	4 to 8	0.1 to 0.5
96 to 128	16 to 24	2 to 4	up to 0.1
64 to 96	12 to 16	1 to 2	

© VAISALA

ALLERGENS

It's hard to play softball outdoors if you're constantly sneezing and your eyes are itchy. But that's the reality for allergy sufferers who venture outdoors in the spring and summer. And global warming is making it worse. Studies show that with rising temperatures, pollen season begins earlier and lasts about 20 days longer in the United States than when your parents were teenagers. On top of that, plants produce more pollen in warmer weather. Pollen counts in 2040 are expected to be more than double what they were in 2000, meaning people with allergies might not be able to go outdoors on bad days.

ASTHMA

Air pollution is a problem for students at schools around the world. Fumes from cars and trucks and even construction make it hard to breathe on a good day. Add global warming to the mix and it can be more dangerous—especially for the five million children under age 18 who suffer from asthma. A chronic lung condition, asthma is also expensive. American families with kids who need inhalers could expect to pay about $3,000 per person a year, according to the US Centers for Disease Control and Prevention.

GARBAGE AND POLLUTION

Marathon swimmers, windsurfers and sailors were told to keep their mouths closed when competing in the 2016 Olympics in Rio de Janeiro, Brazil. That's because ocean waters were so polluted with raw sewage and garbage that athletes risked getting bacterial infections and other illnesses. "Foreign athletes will literally be swimming in human [poop], and they risk getting sick from all those micro-organisms," local doctor Daniel Becker

SCORE!

Professional football (soccer) organizations are starting to educate the next generation of players. In 2021 Planet League got 49 community organizations involved in "scoring points" to win the championship. Participants didn't have to kick the ball into a net to win. Instead they earned points for their club by completing green activities like eating a meat-free meal, walking to school and recycling. In the end, Cambridge United won football's biggest climate tournament. During the first year of the tournament, more than 14,300 climate actions took place, reducing carbon emissions by about 249,000 pounds (113,000 kilograms), which equals planting 6,450 trees.

Our changing climate means more children suffer from asthma, and those children have a harder time breathing when they play sports.
SARRA22/GETTY IMAGES

told the *New York Times* before those games. "It's sad but also worrisome." Since then the Brazilian government has been trying to clean up its act. New projects aim to collect and treat 90 percent of Rio's sewage by 2033.

HERE COMES THE SUN

We need the ozone layer to protect us from the sun's harmful ultraviolet (UV) rays. But because of global warming, the ozone layer is thinner in some areas than it used to be. This means the chances of getting a sunburn—or worse—are higher at certain times of the year. A rating system called the *UV index* lets us know how strong the sun's rays are and how quickly our skin and eyes might be damaged. A rating of 0 indicates low risk, but a 10 means you need to be very careful if you're out in the sun. Scientists are trying to understand whether record-setting heat waves in parts of Europe are happening more often because of holes in the ozone layer. Thanks to international agreements like the **Montreal Protocol**, the world has been phasing out ozone-eating chemicals like those found in aerosol deodorants and refrigerants used to freeze ice rinks. The NHL is shooting to set an example for the 4,800 indoor ice rinks across North America. Instead of using ozone-depleting chlorodifluoromethane (HCFC-22), they're encouraging older facilities to consider using natural refrigerants, such as ammonia or CO_2, both of which are naturally occurring refrigerants with zero ozone-depleting potential.

ON THIN ICE

Wilfrid Laurier University geographer Colin Robertson has been studying the relationship between rising temperatures and the ability of Canadians to skate outdoors. He's been collecting data through a project called RinkWatch to predict how climate change is affecting this winter pastime. By asking skaters to send in information about when they can skate and comparing it to daily temperatures, Robertson estimates that the number of days averaging 23°F (-5°C)—the magic temperature for perfect outdoor ice-skating conditions—will decrease by two weeks by 2040, from 72 days today to just 60 days. It means the average length of the skating season may shrink by 33 percent in eastern Canada, and by 20 percent in western Canada.

DANGER! THIN ICE

Global warming means children might not get to ski on real snow in the future.

IMGORTHAND/GETTY IMAGES

S'NO MORE SNOW

Millions of people in North America enjoy sports like cross-country skiing, downhill skiing and snowboarding. But global warming means higher-than-normal temperatures, unpredictable weather, less snow and even slushy snow. University of Waterloo professor Daniel Scott led a study that looked at the average February daytime temperatures in cities that have already hosted the Olympic Winter Games. He and his international team of researchers discovered that temperatures have increased significantly from the 1920s to the 2000s. By 2100 only one of the 21 Winter Olympics host cities will have the right winter conditions to host the Olympics.

Scott and researchers from Canada, the United States and Austria have looked at how winters have warmed over the last several decades. By looking at the average February daytime temperatures in former Olympic host cities, they found that temperatures have increased by:

0.72°F (0.4°C) from the 1920s to 1950s

5.6°F (about 3.1°C) in the 1960s through 1990s

11°F (about 6.1°C) in Games held in the 21st century, including Beijing in 2022

Unless more is done to keep temperatures from climbing, experts believe the climate will warm by 3.6 to 7°F (2 to 3.9°C) in the 21st century. It would be enough to change life as we know it. Many athletes are already noticing changes. And they're worried that skiing will disappear altogether. Paralympic alpine skier Thomas Walsh is worried. "Who's to know how much longer we'll be able to compete in alpine skiing?" he says. "Not to be pessimistic about it, but there's the question of how long we'll be able to do this, and how long we'll be able to ski outside on real snow."

TRADITIONS FORCED TO CHANGE COURSE

When you think of Alaska, what's the first thing that comes to mind? Snow. Lots of snow. Yet even in the far north, the weather is being affected by climate change. In fact, Alaska is warming up faster than any other state—at more than twice the global rate. The impact is being felt on the Iditarod Trail Sled Dog Race. This 1,000-mile (1,610-kilometer) race across Alaska's snowy wilderness has been testing participants' endurance, grit and perseverance for over 50 years. But recently ideal snow conditions have been replaced by rain, which can quickly freeze and turn trails to ice.

Running on dirt and ice is dangerous for the dogs, and recently many dogs overheated on sunny afternoons and vomited. In 2020 unseasonably warm conditions even flooded parts of the trail. After racing for nearly 10 days, dog teams had to be rescued just 25 miles (40 kilometers) from the finish line. Alaska's most popular sport, the Iditarod is meant to preserve the traditions and culture of Alaska's Indigenous Peoples, but some wonder how much longer it will be before the race doesn't exist at all.

An organization called Protect Our Winters (POW) is determined to slow climate change for the 50 million people who love being outdoors in the winter—from skiers and snowboarders to trail runners and mountain bikers. Made up of athletes, scientists and business leaders, this not-for-profit organization wants to make sure future generations get to experience winter too. Members are training ambassadors, influencing government policy and working with business leaders to secure a stable climate for everyone. We'll see how POW and other organizations are changing sports in the chapters ahead.

Even sled-dog races in Alaska are affected by global warming. Some parts of the course can get slushy, which makes it dangerous.

MDCOOPER/GETTY IMAGES

CHAPTER THREE

SPORTS ARE GETTING GREENER

A recent global survey asked young people what they thought about climate change and the future. Seventy-five percent said the future is frightening, and more than half worry that there's no hope. But many also feel optimistic. With so much change underway to fight global warming—including in the sports world—you might say we're on the offensive.

RAISING THE ROOF

When the Rogers Centre, home stadium of MLB's Toronto Blue Jays, needed a new retractable roof, builders decided to reuse the old one, saving 460,000 square feet (42,735 square meters) of vinyl from ending up in the landfill. The old material was recycled and used to put a new roof over the

Builders of the Rogers Centre in Toronto reused materials when its new roof was built.

MARY MARGARET PERALTA/DREAMSTIME.COM

MetLife Stadium uses a ring of solar panels to produce cleaner energy to help power the arena. That's a touchdown, if you ask me!

heads of 50,000 cheering fans. The team is committed to keeping as much waste out of the landfill as possible:

> Staff is trained to separate recyclables from garbage.

> All food packaging and cutlery is recyclable or can be composted.

> Extra untouched food is donated to the food rescue organization Second Harvest to feed the community.

In 2022 the Jays received the MLB's Green Glove Award for the American League East. As they say in Toronto, "Let's go, Blue Jays!"

SOAKING UP THE SUN

MetLife Stadium, which hosts the New York Jets and New York Giants, has a special power-generating system on its roof called the Solar Ring. The 1,350 *solar panels* power the stadium's *LED lighting*, display system and everyday electricity needs. Lincoln Financial Field, where the Philadelphia Eagles play, has over 11,000 solar panels covering its parking lot and the south side of its stadium. Altogether, their green energy initiatives provide four times the energy needed to power all 10 home games each season.

NO MORE MOWERS

Many organizations use gas-powered lawn mowers to maintain everything from baseball diamonds and cricket pitches to golf courses. But that's starting to change. Some clubs are turning to electric-powered or solar mowers. But at Sonoma Raceway in California, there's an even more environmentally friendly solution. For many years now a flock of sheep has been hard at work weeding and trimming the grass around the IndyCar racetrack. Called the Wooly Weeders, the sheep munch away on the 1,600 acres (647 hectares) of land, fertilizing as they go. The size of the flock ranges from about 650 in winter to 2,500 in summer. People can even "adopt a sheep" to help raise money for children's charities.

EAT TO DEFEAT

HOW MUCH WATER IS NEEDED TO PRODUCE FOOD?

FOOD	QUANTITY	WATER CONSUMPTION (LITERS)
Chocolate	1 kg	17,196
Beef	1 kg	15,415
Cheese	1 kg	3,178
Rice	1 kg	2,497
Bread	1 kg	1,608
Pizza	1 unit	1,239
Apple	1 kg	822
Milk	1 x 250 ml glass	255
Tea	1 x 250 ml cup	27

DATA SOURCE: INSTITUTION OF MECHANICAL ENGINEERS (IME)

When the Forest Green Rovers, an English football (soccer) club, first introduced an all-*vegan* menu in 2015, fans were upset. They even threatened to hire a food truck to serve meat outside the stadium. But then fans tried the food—burgers, pies, sausage rolls and fries. It was delicious—and none of it was made with animal products. Now everyone from fans to players, and even people from other clubs, are smacking their lips and asking for more.

Eating a ***plant-based diet*** is better for the planet because it takes less resources to grow food than to raise animals. Going vegan also improves how athletes feel and perform, and it allows spectators to eat healthier on game days. The Forest Green Rovers isn't just the first vegan football team but is also known as the world's greenest football club. Here's why:

> The stadium has solar panels on its roof and uses wind energy to create additional power.

> The team has three kinds of game jerseys. One is made from bamboo, another is made from recycled plastic, and the third is made from recycled coffee beans and plastic.

> The grass is mowed by a solar-powered robot lawn mower.

> Rainwater is collected and used to water the soccer field.

Athletes play on a field of grass grown organically without pesticides or harmful fertilizers.

A beehive and wildflower plantings support biodiversity.

Young fans have a chance to run around the stadium before every home game. A guide teaches them ways they can care for the planet.

Work has begun on a carbon-neutral football stadium. Called Eco Park, it will be made almost entirely from wood, a low-carbon renewable building material. The grounds will have 500 trees, more than a mile (1.8 kilometers) of shrubs, and meadows to keep local wildlife happy. There will be public transport nearby and electric-car charging stations, and the stadium will be powered by *clean energy*. Of course, all the food will still be vegan!

"Each year we look at what we do," explains Paula Brown, who works for the organization. "We are leading the way and want to be renowned as the club that's doing things differently." This football organization is showing others how it's possible to live sustainably on and off the field.

"WE HAVE TO ACT NOW AND INSPIRE PEOPLE TO JOIN OUR JOURNEY TO SAVE THE PLANET."

—Paula Brown, Forest Green Rovers

TACKLING FOOD WASTE

In 2022 the Minnesota Twins franchise was awarded MLB's Green Glove Award for the 2021 season. It kept almost 100 percent of waste out of the landfill. One of the biggest things it did to earn this title was partner with an organization called Rock and Wrap It Up! to donate more than 10 tons (9 metric tons) of food to local charities each season. In all, the team has kept more than 63 tons (57 metric tons) of waste out of local landfills. Many other professional teams are also taking uneaten food and donating it to people who need it, rather than letting it go to waste.

ALL HANDS ON DECK

World Sailing, the governing body for the sport, is concerned about ocean pollution and is making new rules to make sailing easier on the planet. Talk about making waves!

MICHAEL KAI/GETTY IMAGES

World Sailing is committed to protecting the oceans. Within the next few years, the governing body will require 90 percent of a boat's weight to come from recyclable materials. When

ADVICE FROM A PRO

HOW GOLF IS DRIVING CHANGE

Lee Spivak helps professional golf tournaments fight "fore" the planet. One tournament he's especially proud of is the WM Phoenix Open. Held in Scottsdale, Arizona, every February, the PGA Tour event is called "The Greenest Show on Grass" thanks to its *zero-waste* philosophy. "Golf uses resources to put on a show, like any sport," says Spivak. "People travel to get there, you have to set up the venue, then you use fuel and water and produce a lot of materials during the tournament."

On this big a stage, with fans and media watching, Spivak says the tournament is a chance to show the world that it's possible for golf and all sporting events to keep sustainability in mind. "We're using this tournament as a platform to talk about our own footprint and to educate people about what they can do at home and at work for the climate," he says. "It's an opportunity we don't want to waste." Speaking of waste, here's how the entire team behind the WM Phoenix Open is taking a swing at climate change:

- TPC Scottsdale—the course where the tournament takes place—uses only reclaimed water, which is wastewater that is collected and treated so it can be used for other purposes, such as watering golf courses. TPC Scottsdale also stopped watering certain hills to save water. The dry grass is now golden instead of green.
- Handwashing stations have been replaced by hand-sanitizing stations. Water from cooking and cleaning is used for portable restrooms. In 2022 the organization hit a record and reused 12,000 gallons (45,425 liters) of water during the tournament.
- Bins are provided so everyone from fans to staff know where to put *compostable* products and where to put recyclables.
- There aren't any products in wrappers, like candy, chocolate and cookies, so nothing goes to the landfill.
- Drinks are served in reusable plastic cups that people can take home. Empty wine bottles are collected and transformed into reusable drinking glasses (a process called *upcycling*).
- Many products in the tournament's gift shop, from T-shirts to those funny-looking golf pants, are made from recycled material.
- Leftover food from the tournament is donated to local food banks.
- All construction materials used in the tournament, such as signage and bleachers, are separated and either recycled, donated or reused.
- The tournament uses electric golf carts and e-vehicles on-site. Shuttle buses for fans run partly on biofuel.

"We track and report our greenhouse gas emissions," says Spivak, whose company is teaching other sports organizations how to do the same. He is also optimistic about the future. "Events like ours have a huge ripple effect. We are minimizing our event footprint, but the influence of our impact is larger."

The sailing world is taking sustainability seriously and making changes to help the planet.

BLASTREACH/GETTY IMAGES

it comes to building boats, the organization wants to cut waste in half too. Companies are developing electric boat engines that run on **renewable energy**, so they don't need oil. Sailors are also doing as much as they can to prevent waste from ending up in the landfill or in the ocean. For example:

World Sailing participants wear bibs that resist water and are colored so spectators can see where a sailor is from and if they're leading the race. Now 80 percent of each bib is made from plastic collected at the beach.

In 2016 local craftspeople in Kenya built a dhow (a type of boat) made of plastic collected from beaches and roadsides. They used more than 11 tons (10 metric tons) of plastic waste and 30,000 flip-flops. Called the Flipflopi, the boat has been sailing across Africa, teaching people about **single-use plastics** and how to take care of the oceans.

At the 2019 Miami World Cup, sailors brought their old or damaged wetsuits, which were then turned into yoga mats.

Many sailors are sustainability ambassadors. Paddy Hutchings, a young sailor from the United Kingdom, is one of them. With his #Sail4Sustainability project, he's made it his mission to educate students about plastic pollution, and when he speaks to them he wears Gill marine clothing made from recycled plastic.

PLANNING FOR THE FUTURE

Ninety-five percent of the Paris 2024 Summer Olympic Games are taking place at venues that already exist. Visitors can walk from beach volleyball at the Eiffel Tower to cycling on the Champs-Élysées to fencing at the Grand Palais.

But there's more:

Activities take place in the center of Paris. Everyone is able to get there by train, bike or on foot. In fact, 73 percent of spectators are just a 30-minute bike ride away.

Eighty-five percent of athletes are within 30 minutes of where they're competing. Once in the Olympic Village, zero-emission electric vehicles shuttle them around.

Renewable energy powers the Games.

Anything built is certified as low-carbon, and 95 percent of construction waste can be reused or recycled.

Thirty-two acres (13 hectares) of land was spruced up with greenery, and parts of the Seine were cleaned up so people could swim in it. Recovered water helped plant trees.

The Games have a zero-waste policy, so the goal is that nothing will go to the landfill.

Spectators are part of the action. By eating vegetarian meals or taking public transportation, they earn points for their country. Organizers hope that by spreading the message during the Games, people will continue to live more sustainably when they go home.

Paris is the perfect place for a more centralized Olympics that will make it possible for athletes to walk to their events.

GLOBALP/GETTY IMAGES

FROM VEGAN VOLLEYBALLS TO SUSTAINABLE SURFBOARDS

Athletes like Sarah Hanffou, a French-Cameroonian table tennis player, are taking sustainability seriously. She's recycling Ping-Pong tables and equipment by giving them to developing countries in Africa. Meanwhile, many companies are working on creating greener sports equipment, like biodegradable golf balls with fish food inside. Eco Sports has another solution. It makes basketballs, footballs, volleyballs and baseball gloves out of a biodegradable, recyclable and vegan material. That's good news, since the company says 35,000 cowhides are used to make NFL footballs every year. The surfing industry is getting on board too. Over one million surfboards are made each year, and each one contributes roughly 400 pounds (181 kilograms) of carbon dioxide thanks to the petroleum-based materials used to make it. Today surfboard designers are recycling old boards and reshaping them into new ones—or into skateboards. Even volleyball is serving up change. The International Volleyball Federation's Good Net Project pulls old fishing nets out of the ocean and remakes them into volleyball nets.

COOLER CLOTHES

Thanks to a special partnership with EcoAthletes, Loopt Foundation is working with athletes to champion

HIT OR MISS?

Sports equipment uses natural resources and energy. Every football (soccer ball), for example, is made of plastic (from petroleum), rubber (synthetic or from plants), cotton (from plants) and animal products (like leather). These materials are processed in factories and affect the environment adversely. Take care of your ball so it can last longer. Don't leave it outside in the rain, and don't sit or stand on it. Do play on grass or clay. When you're done with your ball, reuse or donate it. You can even cut a soccer ball in half and upcycle it into a planter!

a social media campaign called #clothes4good. "Athletes are the most influential people on the planet," says Scott Welch, executive director of the Loopt Foundation. "Many of these athletes realize they have a responsibility to make sustainability cool. We need clothes for performance and protection, but what we do with them after really matters." When it comes to clothes, Loopt teaches young people and athletes to think about the following:

HIT OR MISS?

Some estimates say the average American purchases over 59 pieces of clothing a year.
Our consumption of clothing has risen by 400 percent in the last two decades.
The average American does not wear 50 percent of the clothing in their closet.
At the end of its life cycle, about 85 percent of our clothing ends up in a landfill.
In all, the apparel industry produces 10 percent of global greenhouse gas emissions.

1. How many clothes do I buy every year? How many of them do I wear all the time? How do I usually get rid of them? Am I buying sustainable brands that are **B Corp**, organic or **fair trade**?
2. Before you buy, ask yourself if the item fits, if you love it and when or where you will wear it.
3. Choose quality over quantity. You will wear the piece more and it will last longer. Also consider buying secondhand clothes. These are better for your budget and the planet.
4. Care for your clothes by wearing them many times, washing them in cold water and hanging them to dry. Donate clothes when they no longer fit rather than throwing them out.
5. Learn more and share your knowledge with others. A great thing you can do is spread the word!

EcoAthletes like beach volleyball player Melissa Humana-Paredes are getting involved in ensuring that sports clothing is more sustainable.
PETR TOMAN/ALAMY STOCK PHOTO

SCORE!

On a recent plane trip, my coffee was served in a special cup made with 50 percent recycled materials. It keeps hands cool and coffee hot, so you don't need to use a sleeve or double up on cups. Since 63 percent of adults drink coffee every day, simple solutions like this help cut back on the more than 50 billion plastic-lined paper cups that are thrown away each year.

CAN AIRLINES GO GREEN?

We've read about sustainable transportation solutions, from solar-powered sailboats to organizing the Olympics in smarter locations, but what about air travel? Flying creates about 3 percent of global carbon dioxide emissions a year. Many airlines are promising to become carbon-neutral within the next few years. They're experimenting with cleaner fuels and lighter materials to reduce the amount of jet fuel they need. But until that happens, passengers can reduce their carbon "wingprint."

Fly economy—the seats are close together, so the amount of fuel per person is smaller. You can calculate your flight's emissions at gol-calculator.moss.earth.

Take a plane with more seats. A fuller plane emits less emissions per person.

When it's possible, take direct flights rather than flights with stopovers. A lot of emissions happen during takeoff and landing.

Travel light—the less luggage you bring, the less fuel is needed to carry all the extra weight.

Bring your own reusable water bottle and snacks from home for the plane ride. All those airline cups and plastic-wrapped airline meals create garbage.

There are ways to make flying more sustainable. Some airlines are trying to offset carbon emissions, but even things like offering digital tickets and boarding passes instead of printing them makes traveling by air a little better for the planet.
OSCAR WONG/GETTY IMAGES

USING THEIR INFLUENCE FOR GOOD

Fans look up to athletes, so it's great when athletes use their influence to effect change. Many are speaking up about the planet. Here are a few amazing examples:

The MLB's Brent Suter says climate change affects every athlete's on-field performance, and he's encouraging his teammates and fans to get involved in helping the planet.

Shocked by the amount of plastic she sees in the streets, California-born pro soccer player Arianna Criscione makes sure her team works only with environmentally focused brands. She wants to lead by example and save the planet from a problem that "drives her bonkers."

Ice-hockey player Mike Völlmin was frustrated to learn about his carbon footprint—the one he makes by driving and flying hours each week to play hockey. He decided to change the locker-room talk to things like transportation emissions.

Italian sailor Camilla Morelli realized how much fabric goes to waste when one sailboat switches big swaths of fabric sails for another. She decided to recycle that material and founded a company called Camoz, where she upcycles that fabric into fashionable bags. Many other sailors are "jumping on board" with similar ideas.

Many athletes are learning about climate change and speaking out on behalf of the planet. They are using their influence to change the way others think about the environment—and showing that we can make a difference when we all work together.

VICTOR VELTER/SHUTTERSTOCK.COM

Erin Silver

After Justice Bartley took a university course on climate, the former University of Virginia basketball player says his eyes were opened. Upon seeing photos of blazing wildfires in the Amazon, he decided to speak up too. Now an NBA employee, he's teaching the league what he's learned.

J BRARYMI/GETTY IMAGES

LEW BLAUSTEIN

ECOATHLETES

EcoAthletes is a nonprofit organization led by GreenSportsBlog.com founder Lew Blaustein. It's teaching world champions how to be eco champions. This includes how to talk about helping the planet even if they must use planes to get to competitions. I spoke to Blaustein about EcoAthletes and how he got it up and running.

What kinds of issues do you tackle with GreenSportsBlog?

*I cover **LEED-certified** stadiums, zero-waste games, athletes and things like greenwashing, which is when a company says it's green but it's a sham or oversold. Over the last few years, I've found that the sports world is becoming greener, but we can and need to do more to address climate change.*

SCORE!

Green Sports Day is held on October 6 to highlight sustainability in sports around the world. Organizations like Green Sports Alliance, Sports for Climate Action, Players for the Planet, EcoAthletes and others high-five each other online and hold events in person to raise awareness.

Organizations like Players for the Planet are working together to help preserve and protect the earth.

COURTESY OF PLAYERS FOR THE PLANET

What more can sports do to deal with climate change?

Sometimes big sports sponsors are big polluters. Sports organizations can be afraid to speak up because they don't want to cross those sponsors. Athletes have told me they don't talk about climate change, even though they'd like to, because it's too sciencey, they don't want to be called hypocrites for their large personal carbon footprints and/or because climate change can be a political issue. Sports fans are passionate, but athletes move the needle. I created a nonprofit so athletes could lead climate action. That's how EcoAthletes came to be.

What have your athletes accomplished so far?

I started EcoAthletes to take athletes from climate-curious to climate leaders. So far we have 87 champions, and our site features inspirational stories about how their personal health was impacted by climate change, and even how climate change impacted their ability to play their sport. Many athletes are now even working with their teams or leagues to help make their sports more sustainable.

CHAPTER FOUR

SETTING SUSTAINABLE GOALS

Without a crystal ball, it's hard to predict the future. How will athletes train and compete in weather that's too hot? Can we make our gear greener? What can stadiums do to be more sustainable? Thanks to innovations in everything from technology to sneakers, we're starting to see how sports are shaping up for the future.

FORECAST FOR THE FUTURE

Researchers at Arizona State University have tried to predict how high temperatures could go by the end of the century. In a worst-case scenario, temperatures could increase exponentially. The

New technology, such as smartwatches and specialized clothing, can help people train smarter and more safely.
MIREYA ACIERTO/GETTY IMAGES

51

cities that could expect the highest increases in heat exposure include:

Orlando, Florida—up to 126 times more exposure

Austin, Texas—up to 116 times more exposure

Atlanta, Georgia—up to 94 times more exposure

Tampa, Florida—up to 88 times more exposure

Tallahassee, Florida—up to 86 times more exposure

Athletes are learning how to adapt to harsher climates. It's difficult and takes time, but it can really help athletes compete in hotter temperatures.

JORDAN SIEMENS/GETTY IMAGES

These kinds of concerns have researchers trying to figure out how to help athletes survive the elements.

TRAINING FOR TOUGH CONDITIONS

Since at least the 1930s, sports scientists have been studying how athletes can perform better in different kinds of weather. Yannis Pitsiladis is a professor of sport and exercise at the University of Brighton in the United Kingdom. He's seen athletes fall over in high heat and humidity and says it's the best-prepared athletes—not the favorites—who win in extreme conditions. In fact, training properly can increase performance by 5 percent—enough to break world records.

Training for the elements is called ***acclimating***. Some athletes travel to where they will be competing to train. Sometimes athletes can exercise in an environmental chamber—a hot room that simulates heat and humidity—to prepare their bodies for competition. Too few athletes are acclimating for competition. This may help explain why, in 2021, some athletes suffered in the extreme conditions at the Tokyo Olympics.

As we learned in chapter 2, organizers are trying to help. Races are being switched to cooler times and less-humid locations, and competitions are being canceled if conditions aren't safe. Trainers are realizing the importance of cooling down an athlete's body temperature quickly with things like cold baths to prevent them from getting really sick—or worse. Scientists have even created an ingestible "thermometer pill" that wirelessly transmits an athlete's core body temperature. In the future, inventions like this could help coaches know when a player is in danger before it's too late.

> **HIT OR MISS?**
>
> Before the Tokyo Olympics, organizers paved the marathon course with tiny ceramic heat-reflecting beads. Called Perfect Cool, this shimmery gray material was supposed to make it easier for runners to compete in the heat. Races were even scheduled before sunrise! The technology couldn't be tested, though, as the races were switched to a cooler city miles away. In a lower-tech attempt to beat the heat, organizers tried to cool off fans at a canoeing event with shaved ice—spectators got soaked.

CHILLING OUT

If you're watching sports on TV, you might see athletes gulping electrolyte drinks. But these days, that isn't enough. Special equipment is being developed to help athletes keep their bodies at a core temperature of between 97 and 99°F (36.1 and 37.2°C). The science behind it is called ***thermoregulation***. Some football players in the NFL, for instance, use special arm sleeves and helmet liners to keep them cooler. One company makes an instant cooling towel that absorbs sweat and lowers

body temperature. Some specialty clothes can be worn to run marathons. A brand called Solumbra makes a jacket with air vents and fabric that's rated 100+ UPF to protect runners in the sun. A hat developed by a company called Hammacher Schlemmer for use by soldiers helps athletes keep their heads cooler than the air temperature for several hours. Some athletes train for long distances with a hydration vest. This contraption is like a lightweight backpack filled with water, so athletes can drink on the go. In addition to cooling clothes, technology companies are developing apps and wrist monitors so athletes and trainers can monitor body temperature.

CARBON-EATING CLOTHES

A research institute in Hong Kong is experimenting with new fabrics to keep athletes cool—fabrics that can actually absorb carbon from the atmosphere. Researchers at the Hong Kong Research Institute of Textiles and Apparel Limited say that cellulosic yarn can be used to make fabrics that help reduce carbon dioxide levels in the environment. Some products may even be able to absorb the same amount as a tree in a day.

VEGAN RUNNING SHOES

As a former professional football (soccer) player in the Premier League, Michael Doughty didn't discuss issues like the environment with his team. He wasn't allowed. "We were told to keep controversy to a minimum," explains Doughty, now a runner. The more research he did, the more interested he became in sustainability and the environment. It wasn't long before he began championing those values to his friends, family and anyone he met. Doughty also began to worry about the soccer gear he was wearing. He discovered that if the footwear industry were a country, it would be the 17th-largest polluter.

The production of running shoes contributes to global greenhouse gas emissions. Some companies are trying to change that.

EDWIN TAN/GETTY IMAGES

"Almost all [sportswear] products are made using fossil-fuel-derived materials, and it's no secret now that fossil-fuel use is one of the main contributors to the climate crisis," he explains.

In 2020 Doughty founded a high-performance shoe company called Hylo Athletics. Hylo makes a range of shoes with a low-carbon footprint. They are certified vegan, made with renewable materials like sugarcane, corn and algae. "Our mission is clear—to replace all fossil-fuel material use with renewables," says Doughty. "We're not there yet, but we've made some awesome progress so far, and we're excited about the road ahead."

Hylo also has a shoe-recycling program called Hyloop. The company takes back old Hylo shoes to be ground up and used in future products. It even recycles trainers from other companies. Doughty is striving for a future where athletes don't have to sacrifice performance for impact—a future where athletes can champion environmentally friendly products and influence positive change. With a roster of professional athletes on board and slogans like "Run like the world depends on it" and "The future is still ours to write," Hylo is in it to win it.

SHOES YOU'LL NEVER OWN

One Swiss sports brand is so happy with its invention that it's walking on cloud nine. Called On, the company has designed the first shoe made from carbon emissions. They've named it Cloudprime, and it's made from a new foam material called CleanCloud. With help from partners at every stage, the company captures carbon emissions from industrial sources like steel mills or landfill sites before they're released into the air. The emissions are turned into a liquid and then dehydrated and turned into the kind of foam needed to cushion shoes.

Companies like On are making more-sustainable running shoes. On has a model that's made from carbon emissions.

COURTESY OF ON

But that's not all On has done for the planet. The company also launched the world's first *circular* high-performance running shoe. Called Cloudneo, the shoe has an upper made from a lightweight material derived from castor beans. Subscribers pay a monthly fee, and six months after their purchase, customers can return their used shoes and get another pair. Once returned, the shoes are recycled and turned into new running gear. It's a great example of circularity—the product will get used over and over and never go to waste. On calls it "the shoe you will never own." Their hope is that, in the not-too-distant future, people will be surprised to learn that people once owned their shoes.

SOMETHING TO CHEW ON

Manchester City Football Club in England is kicking single-use plastics to the curb. But instead of a plastic-bottle ban, the soccer team experimented with a whole new idea—coffee cups you can actually eat. Made of natural ingredients like wheat flour and oat bran, they are similar to wafers or a cone. The cups keep drinks hot and stay crunchy for 40 minutes, or almost half a soccer game. When they're done drinking their beverages, fans can eat their cups. Several companies are now producing cups like these and hope they can be used for everything from coffee and soup to ice cream and yogurt—and not just at Manchester City's Etihad Stadium either. They're hoping to sell to places like restaurants, offices and more stadiums around the world.

THE FUTURE OF HOCKEY

With many players learning to skate on ponds and in backyard rinks, the future of hockey is on thin ice. The NHL knows that hockey needs to get greener and lead by example if the game is going to be played in the years ahead. With this in mind, the NHL began rolling out a series of green initiatives. One of its most creative ways to ensure hockey can be played into the future is the annual Future Goals Virtual Science Fair, a competition co-sponsored by the NHL and the National Hockey League Players' Association (NHLPA). For a recent fair, students were asked to submit projects for redesigning an element of a hockey arena to make it more environmentally sustainable.

Winners had some great ideas. Each first-place winner received $2,500 US for a sustainable project at their school. Langstyn V. from Massachusetts researched operational improvements such as using LED light bulbs and recyclable low-density polyethylene thermoplastics (plastic that can be reshaped many times) instead of plexiglass for rink boards. Tyler K. from Minnesota studied

SCORE!

Patagonia is a Certified B Corporation that sells sustainable outdoor clothing and sports equipment. Worried about climate change and determined to do more, Patagonia founder Yvon Chouinard and his family transferred ownership of the company to a fund that will be used to fight climate change. If things go well, Patagonia will give $100 million a year to fight climate change.

HIT OR MISS?

Some companies or stadiums buy carbon credits, which are essentially permits that allow them to emit a certain amount of carbon dioxide or other greenhouse gases and offset it by such things as planting trees or paying another company to reduce its emissions or capture its carbon. In this way, the total carbon footprint is reduced. Experts hope that by 2050, 90 percent of the world's electricity can come from renewable energy and carbon credits won't be needed. They agree this is just a temporary solution until more companies can find ways to use reduce their emissions.

SCORE!

Before Climate Pledge Arena opened, the owners were committed to diverting 95 percent of the waste generated at events away from a landfill. The staff at the arena quickly realized that this ambitious waste goal could not be achieved without sorting through every single bag of garbage. "During every event and game, housekeeping staff sort through every bin to ensure every material is diverted to the correct stream," says Brianna Treat, director of sustainability at Climate Pledge Arena. "They split open every bag to ensure each piece went into the proper waste stream." Within a few months, they hit their highest diversion rate of 98 percent, higher than the arena's monthly goal. Way to go, team!

IN THE SPOTLIGHT

CLIMATE PLEDGE ARENA

As the director of sustainability at Seattle's Climate Pledge Arena, the world's first *zero-carbon* stadium, Brianna Treat has an important job. "Climate Pledge Arena was named after a vision, not a corporation," says Treat, who works at the stadium that hosts the NHL's Seattle Kraken, the WNBA's Seattle Storm and a range of concerts and entertainers. The arena offsets its carbon every year, well ahead of its 2040 goal as a signatory of The Climate Pledge, a group of businesses around the world that have agreed to tackle carbon emissions in their companies. Here are a few of the arena's successes so far:

- The arena diverts more than 95 percent of all its waste, which is considered zero-waste.
- The arena eliminated single-use plastics for beverages, chips and candy.
- In 2022, its first full year of operation, the arena collected more than 180,000 gallons (681,374 liters) of rainwater, enabling it to make some of the greenest ice in the NHL.

Even ice is getting greener. Organizations like the NHL are reducing emissions and reusing resources to create skating rinks and arenas.

SEATTLE KRAKEN

whether raising the freezing point of water using chemicals would lower the amount of energy used to maintain an NHL ice rink.

INNOVATIONS IN RENEWABLE ENERGY

Remember the Forest Green Rovers? The club was owned by a man named Dale Vince, founder of a renewable-energy

- This is the only stadium to run entirely on electricity and be completely fossil-fuel-free. It has a fleet of electric forklifts and golf carts for crew to use and an electric Zamboni. All the energy the stadium needs is from renewable sources like solar and wind energy.
- The arena and the teams it hosts are investing in public transportation and aiming to get at least a quarter of all visitors to take public transportation to the arena. Treat says that everyone with a Kraken or Storm game ticket gets a free transportation pass for two hours before and after the game.
- Fans, including young ones, are being taught how to be more sustainable. "Waste Management brought a recycling truck to the arena during kids' night in April," says Treat. "They played sorting games and taught them how to recycle and compost. It was super cool to see."
- Seattle Kraken's One Roof Foundation brings communities and school groups to the arena so that people who don't typically get introduced to hockey have a chance to see the game.

"TEAMS FROM THE UNITED STATES AND EUROPE ARE CONTACTING US ABOUT HOW WE'RE GOING ZERO-WASTE, BECOMING ALL ELECTRIC AND REDUCING CARBON IN ALL WE DO. THAT WAS THE PURPOSE OF THE ARENA—TO SHOW OTHER ARENAS THAT IT'S POSSIBLE TO ACHIEVE NET-ZERO. WE ARE ALL REALLY PROUD."

—**Brianna Treat**, director of sustainability at Climate Pledge Arena

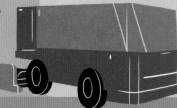

The company Ecotricity created zero-emission cars and superbikes—and boy, are they fast!

ADAM GASSON/ALAMY STOCK PHOTO

company called Ecotricity. He gets credit for turning the football (soccer) organization into the greenest club in the world. He's shown other sports teams that it's possible to be successful and sustainable. Ecotricity created a zero-emission superbike that can go 150 miles per hour (241.40 kilometers per hour). The company also created a sports car to show the world how snazzy you can look in a vehicle powered by green gas.

ESPORTS AND VIDEO GAMES

In recent years, esports have become big business. The market is expected to go from $1.44 billion in 2022 to $5.48 billion in 2029. By then the three biggest markets will be the United States, China and South Korea. So what exactly are esports? The term is short for electronic sports, which are organized, competitive video games that pit participants against one another individually or as part of a team. Players can have contracts and sponsors, and they train at high-tech facilities and even compete at stadiums. Some players are so popular, they're global superstars—just like professional soccer or baseball players.

More than 70 percent of Americans play video games regularly, either on their phones or on gaming systems. The emissions created by gaming in America are equivalent to putting 5 million more cars on the road or plugging in

Esports competitions are more popular than ever, but there are ways to save energy when you play video games at home too.

another 85 million fridges. How does this happen? Gaming systems need electricity, which often comes from burning ***fossil fuels*** like coal and natural gas. Electricity generated by burning coal, oil or gas is nonrenewable—and not good for the planet. In fact, coal and oil are two of the dirtiest kinds of fuel. Energy created using the sun, water (***hydro-electricity***) or wind is renewable and cleaner. If you're into esports, you can reduce your footprint by putting your system into power-saving mode and buying electronics with the Energy Star logo.

Solar energy is clean and renewable. It's being used to generate enough energy to power stadiums and even the electricity in some homes.
YAORUSHENG/GETTY IMAGES

SAILING TOWARD A SUSTAINABLE FUTURE

Ivar Smits and Floris van Hees call themselves Sailors for Sustainability— and they've definitely earned their name. The two Dutch men set sail in 2016 on a trip around the world—and years later they're still at it! The duo is so passionate about the environment that they've been searching for and documenting the most creative and sustainable solutions to climate challenges. By the time they they dock at home, they'll have sailed 70,000 nautical miles and visited 45 countries. I caught up with them during their journey to learn more.

What does sustainability look like on a boat?
SMITS: *We downsized and live on a boat, so we don't have a house or car elsewhere. We've chosen a floating tiny house that uses wind energy instead of fossil fuels to travel around the world to minimize our impact on the environment.*
VAN HEES: *We try to be mindful of waste. Whenever we can, we shop at local markets for packaging-free food. We bring our own containers to avoid waste. We buy local and seasonable and eat mostly plant-based foods. We recycle and produce our own renewable energy with solar panels and a wind generator. It's how we charge our computers and phones and keep the fridge running. We try to limit what we buy and don't have a lot of stuff. It's liberating! We don't really need that much.*

What are you hoping to discover while you're traveling around the world?
VAN HEES: *We focus on positive stories. The list of stories we've documented is very diverse. We've found tiny houses in New Zealand made of recycled materials. The skylight was even made from the escape hatch of an old bus. In Uruguay and Argentina, we learned about sustainable schools with car tires in the playground, a fruit and vegetable garden and walls that are made with glass bottles, cans and tires. We even came across Germany's first package-free grocery store, called Unverpackt, where everyone has to bring their own containers.*

How have things changed since you began this sailing expedition?
SMITS: *When we left over six years ago,* sustainability *wasn't a term you heard every day. We had to explain what it meant. Now you hear it a lot more.*
VAN HEES: *And the alternatives are being put into practice. We think that more people will start adopting these alternative ways because they realize [they're] better for them personally and for the community, globally and future generations. Children especially are keenly aware of what's at stake. It's their future.*

You two have spent a lot of time together. Are you sick of each other yet?
SMITS: *We run this NGO together, sail together and are together a lot. Sometimes that's challenging, but we both are open about our feelings and opinions.*
VAN HEES: *But we have good division of tasks. Ivar is the captain when we're at sea, and I'm the captain on land. We make a great team!*

CHAPTER FIVE

HOW TO BE PART OF THE WINNING TEAM

Just thinking about climate change can feel overwhelming—especially if you're a kid. But there's actually a lot you can do to make sports more sustainable. By making even small changes to your daily routine, and encouraging your teammates to do the same, you can have a big impact. This chapter looks at some of the many ways young athletes are leading the way. You can be a part of the action too.

GREAT RECYCLERS: EYE ON THE PRIZE

Cooper Waisberg is a teenager with a vision. He and his brother are the cofounders of Balls 4 Eyeballs, an organization on a mission to make tennis greener while funding eye research. "After our grandmother was diagnosed with glaucoma, we became eager to find ways to help improve the lives of those suffering from vision loss," explains Waisberg, who

When everyone does their part—even if it's a small part—we can all be part of a winning team.
DSY88/GETTY IMAGES

hopes to become a lawyer one day. He and his brother Ethan, who is studying medicine, have a shared passion. "Both lifelong tennis players, we have seen firsthand that many tennis balls are thrown away every year, ending up in landfill sites," says Waisberg.

Their organization has put collection bins in tennis clubs across Canada so that people can easily donate used tennis balls. So far more than 50,000 of those fuzzy green balls have been kept out of landfills, which equals more than 6,000 pounds (2,721 kilograms) of non-decomposable waste. The proceeds from their initiative are donated to Canadian eye charities like Fighting Blindness Canada, Orbis Canada and Medical Ministry International.

HI-YA EDUCATION: THE NEXT GENERATION

Jadir Taekwondo Association (AJTKD) is a nonprofit martial arts organization in Rio de Janeiro. Leaders there are committed to educating young students, and not just about self-defense. They also go on the offensive, teaching about 80 martial artists aged 5 to 17 how to live more sustainably at home, at school and in sports.

Teaching martial-arts students about the planet is an important part of AJTKD in Brazil.
COURTESY OF AJTKD

"Climate change is one of the most pressing global issues of our time, and sport, with its broad reach and incredible potential to bring people together, plays an important role as part of the solution," says Danilo Malafaia, administrative director at AJTKD. "It can raise awareness, influence behaviors and contribute to creative, low-cost, high-impact solutions."

Myrka Suarez is an environmental educator who works with students at AJTKD. "Environmental action is constant; it's not a one-time activity," she says. "The sooner we teach about the environment, the easier it is to learn about its importance and what actions we can take."

Results can be seen when students bring reusable bottles to class and get groceries with their own shopping bags. "We like to believe that our students do something every day to live a more sustainable life with the knowledge we share with them," says Suarez. "Although the whole responsibility of environmental action does not fall on our shoulders, we teach them that every little action matters."

GREENEST GAME PLAN:
SAVING THE PLANET THROUGH FOOTBALL

When Norwegian football (soccer) player Morten Thorsby was playing for the Heerenveen team in the Netherlands, he convinced the football club to buy bikes for the players. He wanted his teammates to be able to bike from the training complex to the stadium to reduce their carbon footprints. Inspired by that success, he then convinced the team to add solar panels to the stadium roof and asked to have less meat on the club's menu. That's when Thorsby realized he could use football to help save the planet.

Football has a huge following, with a community of more than 3.5 billion people. With that in mind, Thorsby founded a nonprofit organization called We Play Green. By using the influence of professional clubs and players, We Play Green aims to influence others to think more sustainably. To drive his point home further, Thorsby changed his playing number to 2. It represents the world's goal to keep the global temperature from rising by more than 3.6°F (2°C) above pre-industrial levels in order to prevent a climate catastrophe.

BEST IN SNOW:
BOOSTING THE CONVERSATION

Chloe Kim was just 18 when she joined Protect Our Winters as an ambassador. Kim had just become the youngest woman ever to win a gold medal in snowboarding at the Olympics,

SCORE!

We Play Green started the "green bag" project. The organization distributes green bags at professional and recreational football (soccer) clubs across Norway and asks fans to donate used clothing, jerseys and shoes. These items are reused, upcycled or disposed of properly. We Play Green points out that football (soccer) apparel is responsible for 0.4 percent of all global carbon emissions while the fashion industry itself creates about 8 to 10 percent of global emissions.

WE PLAY GREEN

and she wanted to use her platform for the greater good. "Seeing the impacts of climate change firsthand and hearing all of the discussions happening around it, I felt like I needed to get involved," Kim explains. "My career and my love of snowboarding depend on it."

Realizing the need to pick up speed and not "snow" down, she continues to talk about climate change. In Nike's *Talking Trash* podcast, Kim says the climate crisis is affecting her sport and athletes all over the world. Things have changed so much that real snow is now a luxury. She wants to be able to snowboard with her kids someday, and she worries it won't be possible. "I don't want snow to be some prehistoric thing," she says.

SCORE!

Players for the Planet has a new program, and it's "growing" quickly. It's a partnership between fans, professional baseball players and One Tree Planted, a nonprofit that has planted over 40 million trees in 43 countries. Parents can get involved by sponsoring their own children. Every time their Little Leaguer makes a play—say by striking out a batter or getting a base hit—a tree will be planted in their name. You can even root for professional players. Which MLB star will win the Golden Shovel Award this year for planting the most trees?

When athletes such as rock climber Ashima Shiraishi share their personal choices, they hope to effect change. They lead by example, and people like me and you look up to them.
SIMON LEGNER/WIKIMEDIA COMMONS/ CC BY-SA 4.0

MAKING IT PERSONAL: CLIMBING FOR A CAUSE

Ashima Shiraishi was still in middle school when she caught the world's attention by completing some of the most-difficult mountain climbs. When she was 11, she became the youngest person to climb Southern Smoke in Kentucky's Red River Gorge. Since then Shiraishi has won many world climbing championships, and she's even written a children's book. Through it all, she's stuck to her values of living sustainably. She grew up wearing climbing pants made by her mother, and she's now sponsored by a brand that considers the life cycle of clothing. "I like Arc'teryx's emphasis on trying to find ways to repurpose their excess materials from their factories and create something out of it rather than [it] going to waste,"

TREVOR WILLIAMS/GETTY IMAGES

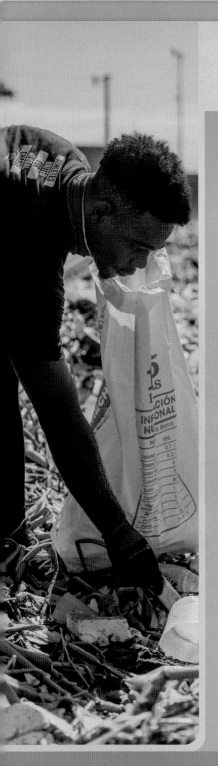

IN THE SPOTLIGHT

IN THE SPOTLIGHT
PLAYERS FOR THE PLANET

After seeing the number of single-use plastic bottles used by professional baseball teams, Chris Dickerson decided to act. An MLB player from 2008 to 2014, he cofounded Players for the Planet in 2007 before he made his big-league debut. His organization hosts a range of programs, from educating young prospects and planting trees to e-waste recycling drives. But his main program—Batting Cleanup—focuses on cleaning up the trash-clogged shoreline at Montesinos Beach in the Dominican Republic (DR).

"The DR is the summation of a broken system," explains Dickerson, who grew up in California and has been interested in the environment from a young age. "There aren't any recycling bins, and people aren't picking up the trash. There's a misunderstanding that it's okay to throw garbage out in a river or waterway so it's carried out of your sight. What they don't realize is that all rivers and waterways lead to oceans and [it] washes back onshore."

Montesinos Beach has become the place where plastic trash piles up—and it's right next to the biggest city in a country where baseball reigns supreme. "It's a weird juxtaposition of a beautiful island country whose coastlines are under a barrage of plastic that constantly washes up on shores every day," he says.

STEPPING UP TO THE PLATE

Every year for the last several years, a growing number of young baseball prospects, major leaguers and even athletes from other sports have come together to clean up the beach and learn more about the plastic problem and what can be done about it. On one recent cleanup mission, 360 participants from seven major-league academies in the DR collected nearly 4.3 tons (3.9 metric tons) of debris. It included:

- 180 pounds (81 kilograms) of glass
- 380 pounds (172 kilograms) of aluminum
- 3,949 pounds (1,791 kilograms) of high-density poly-ethylene plastic
- 8,425 pounds (3821 kilograms) of hard plastics
- 580 pounds (263 kilograms) of styrofoam
- 18 pounds (8 kilograms) of food cartons
- 1,189 pounds (539 kilograms) of discarded shoes
- 2,169 pounds (983 kilograms) of miscellaneous trash

Dickerson is especially proud of the nonprofit's in-person workshops. "We work with the athletes in the DR baseball academies to teach them what plastic is, where it comes from, how it affects us and how it's damaging to the DR and globally." He's also taken things a step further, giving athletes the tools to make an impact, such as reusable water bottles and recycling collection bins. He hopes that using his influence will inspire local communities, and especially young people, to find solutions to the plastic problem.

"Young people are so important, as this is the problem they're inheriting," he says. "Unfortunately the irresponsibility of past generations will be the greatest challenge of this generation's lifetime. There's a sense of urgency to act now, and I'm proud that Players for the Planet can help empower them to act."

(LEFT AND RIGHT)
COURTESY OF PLAYERS FOR THE PLANET

SCORE!

Kai Jones is a young freestyle skiing phenom and the nephew of snowboarder and Protect Our Winters (POW) founder Jeremy Jones. Like his uncle, he wants to effect change—and he's asking adults to step up at election time. "I'm too young to vote, but do me and my generation a favor and vote for climate," says Jones. The teenager works with POW to spread awareness, and he's also taking the lead at school. Based in Wyoming, Jones fundraises for POW at school, and he and his friends bike to school and save energy and water whenever they can.

she says. "It's exciting to be forward-thinking on what clothing can be, while being sustainable and less damaging to our earth." She hopes that by sharing some of her own personal choices, people will be motivated to think about how they can make an impact in their own way too.

HONOR-ROLL STUDENTS: SUSTAINABILITY IN PHYS ED

Sustainability is an essential part of every school subject in Australia and New Zealand—even in gym class. Teachers are finding fun and creative ways to make protecting the planet part of the curriculum. In English, students write persuasive essays about the environment. Geometry lessons can be taught outdoors, and in home economics students use local produce to cook seasonal foods and talk about food waste. Gym teachers use fair-trade footballs and discuss how much water is needed to keep the pitches looking green. Making these connections every day helps students make greener choices so they can protect the planet at lunchtime and in the future. For their efforts to incorporate sustainability into their curriculum, students get an A+!

TINIEST FOOTPRINT: DOING AS MUCH AS SHE CAN

Welsh table-tennis phenom Anna Hursey was just a little girl when she discovered that climate change was affecting

ADVICE FROM A PRO

Ellis Spiezia didn't even have his driver's license when he decided to become a professional electric-race-car driver. Born in Florida, he began racing at indoor go-kart tracks when he was 14. Today he lives in Düsseldorf, Germany, with his parents and races in a new electric race-car series.

He didn't get into racing electric cars with the idea of becoming an eco-champion. "I got into it for the driving. It's what I love to do," Spiezia explains. But over the years, the teen has been able to meet so many people who are passionate about electric vehicle technology, and he was excited to partner with them. "I practice *passive activism*," he says. "I get to do what I'm passionate about—driving race cars—but I also get to showcase awesome EV technology and partner with some amazing brands at the forefront of sustainability. Together we get to help with climate change." Spiezia is proud to partner with brands who share his values. He likes a company called Coorest—it's planting trees in Spain and using technology to ensure that companies are properly counting their carbon credits. In other words, it's making sure that companies who say they're going to make up for their carbon use actually do.

The young racer is happy with the changes underway on the race-track. "I'm seeing a lot of racing circuits in Sweden and Denmark that have a solar grid so cars can charge off the sun or a wind farm," he says. "Small steps like that are happening. Racing is becoming more sustainable."

her health. "I suffer with asthma and know the effects of air pollution personally, but it was my father who has helped me to see the bigger picture of how climate change is affecting us all," Hursey says. That's when she decided to change her life for the greener good. "We started small with using less plastic, less energy and also fewer fossil fuels by walking instead of driving whenever we can."

Today, even with her hectic competition schedule, Hursey lives carbon-neutral as best she can. "I try to produce

Even athletes who must travel to compete can offset their emissions in other ways. Some eat a vegetarian diet at home or use public transportation to get to practices.

as little a carbon footprint as possible," she says. "It is inevitable that I sometimes need to fly to compete, but I try to make it up by contributing toward planting trees and deforestation initiatives."

As a young UN climate ambassador, she encourages others to make simple changes to their daily lives. She tells kids to make even small changes, like turning off the tap when brushing their teeth, switching off lights and gadgets, walking and cycling more and not wasting things. The teen wants others to realize that helping the planet is a team effort. "Only when we realize the earth is getting warmer, the glaciers are melting and sea levels are rising [do] we begin to see our fate as one," she says.

QUICKEST STUDY: KICKING CARBON

As an outdoor field sport, cricket is one of the hardest hit by climate change. That's a problem for Joe Cooke, a professional cricket player. As a student, he always thought climate change was going to happen in the distant future, but when the pitch at Lord's Cricket Ground in England was flooded because of rain, he realized something important: climate change is happening now.

Cooke and his teammates are doing as much as they can to make sure cricket is more sustainable. He's using his university education to help make his club, Glamorgan Cricket, a **net-zero** organization. He also says many players are switching to a vegan diet and encouraging the English and Wales Cricket Board to change their playing schedule to reduce the amount of flying and traveling athletes have to do. He's partnered with many organizations, like EcoAthletes and Friends of the Earth, and he works with sustainable sponsors.

But you don't have to be a famous cricket star to make a difference. "People should educate themselves on small habits as those actions can make a massive difference," he says.

FACING FEARS HEAD-ON: SPEAKING UP FOR THE PLANET

Armenian-born Myroslava "Myra" Fisun began skating competitively when she was in the third grade. But by the time she was in high school in California, injuries and cuts to her school skating program put her on the sidelines. But not for long. She began coaching—and she was good at it. At the same time, Fisun was getting stressed out. "I couldn't avoid the news about climate disasters, with glaciers melting, wildfires and the rest," she says. "It was terrifying, and I ended up with a case of climate anxiety." Looking for a way to take control, she joined a youth-led organization called the Sunrise Movement, in which she helped with research projects and took on major public-speaking roles. In addition to becoming an EcoAthlete, she has now made climate action her full-time job.

Cricket is one of the most popular sports in the world, and famous cricketers are trying to make the sport more sustainable before it's too late.
RAWPIXEL.COM/SHUTTERSTOCK.COM

DON'T SIT ON THE SIDELINES!
10 WAYS TO MAKE YOUR TEAM MORE SUSTAINABLE

There are so many ways you and your team can help protect the planet. Why not bring a reusable water bottle and encourage your teammates and coaches to do the same?

THOMAS BARWICK/GETTY IMAGES

1. Think about your snacks and pre-game meal. Buy seasonal and local, and try a meatless meal once in a while, like the Forest Green Rovers Football Club.

2. Walk, bike, take the bus or carpool to practices and games. It's better for the planet and will get you warmed up to play! Ask your teammates and fans to do the same.

3. Does your ballpark or soccer field use LED lighting or have sensors so that lights shut off automatically when nobody is there? If every house in the United States replaced just one regular bulb with an LED bulb, greenhouse gas emissions would be reduced by as much as 9 billion pounds (4 billion kilograms). Ask your parents for help figuring out who you can speak to about saving energy at your facility.

4. Encourage your team, coaches, parents and the people who run your snack bar to ban single-use plastics and items with wrappers. Bring your own reusable bottle and lead the way.

5. Donate your used equipment and sporting goods. Why not organize a used-equipment sale with the help of your teammates?

6. Talk to your coaches about ordering reversible jerseys, rather than having one for home and another for away games. Does every player need to order a new jersey each year, or can some team-mates still wear their shirt from the year before?

7. Instead of printing game-day tickets or having plastic membership cards to get into facilities, take note of what you can do to reduce waste. Ask about going digital.

8. Clean up after your practices and games. Don't leave garbage lying around. Recycle the glass, tin and plastic you see on the ground.

9. You worked hard in practice and are really sweaty. Keep showers short to avoid wasting water.

10. Be an eco-athlete. No, you don't have to be a pro athlete, but you can share information with your class and teachers at school. Is there anything you can do, even in gym class, to make sports more sustainable?

RACING TO ZERO

Oluseyi Smith is a two-time Canadian Olympian. He competed in track and field and bobsleigh in 2012 and 2018. As an elite athlete and International Olympic Committee Young Leader, he saw how much was happening at the top levels to make sports greener. But at the grassroots level, few organizations were thinking enough about climate change or measuring how their activities were affecting the planet. Smith had to act. He established Racing to Zero in 2022 as a way to help organizations and event organizers, from local clubs to national sports organizations, take action for the planet.

Backed by a team of young Olympians, Racing to Zero is making its mark. "The purpose of this organization is to help community sport achieve its environmental sustainability goals," says Smith, who encourages community sports organizations to think about things like plastic, transportation and other aspects of sustainability.

Racing to Zero helps organizations learn how to lessen their impact on the planet. Smith's long-term dream is to scale up to a point where every country, sport and club can measure its footprint and take next steps. "What I'd say to all young athletes and potential young leaders trying to take a similar path is don't be apathetic," says Smith. "Don't feel like there's nothing you can do. Do something—it doesn't matter how small it is. We should all try to make our communities a little bit better. We all have a part to play."

BE PART OF THE WINNING TEAM!

If you picked up this book, you're likely interested in sports. Maybe you play on a team or at the park with your friends. Maybe you enjoy cheering on your favorite athletes or pro clubs. It's also possible that you're reading this book because you're a fan of the planet who cares about climate change and wants to make a difference. I hope that *In It to Win It* has given you lots of information, ideas and inspiration to get involved. Even the smallest actions add up, just like Smith says. And when we all work together at home, at school or with our teammates, we can make a big difference. We can all play for the planet.

HIT OR MISS?

The more you hear about the climate crisis, the more you worry—especially if you're part of Generation Z, also known as the climate generation. So many young people are worried that the fear has been given a name: climate anxiety, or eco-anxiety. The American Psychological Association calls it a chronic fear of environmental doom. Other feelings can include guilt, grief and overwhelming desperation about the future of the planet. In 2023 Friends of the Earth, an environmental nonprofit, found that more than 66 percent of 18- to 24-year-olds experience climate anxiety. So what can we do about it? Experts say that searching for positive stories about climate change can help. Try to fill your social-media feed with good-news stories about some of the things or people in this book. Taking action, even by donating clothes you don't wear, can help you feel empowered. It's also a good idea to talk about these feelings with an adult you trust.

Working together is one way we can score a goal for the planet. It might not feel like you can make a big impact, but you can, especially when you're part of a team!

THOMAS BARWICK/GETTY IMAGES

GLOSSARY

acclimating—adapting to a new temperature, altitude, climate, environment or situation. Athletes acclimate by training in the environment in which they'll be competing, to get their bodies used to different heat and humidity.

B Corp—certification that indicates a business meets high standards of social and environmental performance, taking care of workers and the planet

biofuel—a kind of fuel made from renewable materials like canola, soy or flax or even animal products like grease and fat

carbon credits—permits that allow companies to emit a certain amount of carbon dioxide and other greenhouse gases and offset it by reducing or removing emissions in other ways or by paying another company to reduce its carbon footprint

carbon dioxide (CO_2) emissions—carbon dioxide released into the air, also referred to as *carbon emissions*

carbon footprint—the total amount of greenhouse gas emissions produced by a person, family, organization, business, etc.

carbon-neutral—a state of net-zero carbon emissions, achieved by balancing the amount of carbon emitted by the amount removed

circular—designed to reduce waste and pollution by keeping products and materials in use for as long as possible, achieved by reusing, repairing or recycling to keep them out of the landfill

clean energy—energy from renewable, zero-emission sources that do not pollute the atmosphere

climate change—a long-term shift in global and regional weather and climate patterns, caused by human activities such as the burning of fossil fuels

climate comeback—phrase that highlights an athlete's positive impact on the planet and helps to inspire others to take action on climate change too

climate crisis—term to describe the urgency of the need to change our behavior to keep the severe adverse effects of global warming and climate change from worsening

climate positive—also called *carbon negative*, this refers to having a positive impact on the environment by removing as much carbon dioxide from the atmosphere as you emit—or more

compostable—capable of decomposing, or decaying, into nutrients that can be returned to the earth

decarbonize—reduce or remove carbon output

erosion—the wearing away of soil or rock by the action of wind, water or ice

fair trade—a global movement that aims to have developed countries pay farmers or producers in developing countries fair prices for their products. It also encourages higher social and environmental standards, including workers being treated fairly.

fossil fuels—nonrenewable fuels such as oil, coal and natural gas, formed over millions of years from decaying plants and animals buried in the earth's crust

global warming—the steady rise in the earth's average surface temperature since the pre-industrial period (1850 to 1900). Human activities have increased this average by 1.9°F (1.1°C). The temperature is increasing by more than 0.36°F (0.2°C) per decade, with consequences already felt around the world.

greenhouse gases—gases in the atmosphere that trap heat and cause the earth's temperature to rise

greenwashing—presenting misleading information that makes a product or company seem more environmentally friendly than it really is

hydrochlorofluorocarbons (HCFCs)/ hydrofluorocarbons (HFCs)—chemical compounds that are commonly used for refrigeration and air-conditioning, including keeping the ice at rinks cold, and which destroy the ozone layer and contribute to climate change

hydroelectricity—electricity produced by the energy of moving water

idle—(verb) leave the engine running while a vehicle isn't moving

LED lighting—light produced using light-emitting diodes (LEDs). LED light bulbs last longer, produce better lighting and are more energy efficient than incandescent bulbs.

LEED-certified—meeting certain sustainability standards in terms of carbon, energy, water, waste and transportation

megadrought—extremely severe drought (dry period) that lasts for many years

microplastics—tiny pieces of plastic, created when plastic products break down, that end up in the environment and harm the environment and animals

Montreal Protocol—an international treaty signed in 1987 in which countries agreed to phase out the production of substances that eat away at the ozone layer

net-zero—a state in which the same amount of greenhouse gas emissions is released as is removed from the atmosphere. (Achieving carbon neutrality means reducing carbon dioxide emissions to net-zero.)

ozone layer—a thin part of the earth's upper atmosphere that acts like a shield by absorbing harmful ultraviolet rays from the sun

passive activism—supporting a cause by participating only when it is easy or convenient, rather than taking genuine action

pesticides—chemicals used to keep bugs from eating plants but which also harm the environment

petroleum—a liquid fossil fuel, also known as *crude oil*, that occurs naturally underground and can be refined to make gasoline, diesel fuel, home heating oil and many other products

plant-based diet—an eating pattern that limits or avoids animal products and focuses on foods from plants, like vegetables, fruits, whole grains, nuts and seeds

renewable energy—energy from natural sources, such as the sun, wind and water, that can be replenished at a higher rate than it is consumed

single-use plastics—plastic items that are used only once before being thrown away, such as water bottles and takeout cutlery

solar panels—arrays of connected solar cells that collect sunlight and turn it into electricity

tailgating—gathering in a parking lot before or after an event like an NFL football game to have a party with food and drinks

thermoregulation—maintenance of an internal body temperature that's not too hot or too cold, both of which can be dangerous

upcycling—transforming unwanted or waste materials into new and better things

vegan—consuming no food that comes from animals, including meat, eggs and dairy products

zero-carbon—creating no carbon emissions

zero-waste—adhering to the principle of generating as little waste as possible, then composting, reusing or recycling any that is produced

RESOURCES

PRINT

Cherry, Lynne. *How We Know What We Know about Our Changing Climate: Scientists and Kids Explore Global Warming.* Dawn Publications, 2010.

Klein, Naomi, and Rebecca Stefoff. *How to Change Everything: The Young Human's Guide to Protecting the Planet and Each Other.* Puffin Canada, 2021.

Miles, David. *Climate Change: The Choice Is Ours: The Facts, Our Future, and Why There's Hope!* Bushel & Peck Books, 2020.

Minoglio, Andrea. *Our World Out of Balance: Understanding Climate Change and What We Can Do.* Blue Dot Kids Press, 2021.

Mulder, Michelle. *Brilliant! Shining a Light on Sustainable Energy.* Paperback edition. Orca Book Publishers, 2016.

ONLINE

Podcasts and Webinars

Nike—Talking Trash: y-u-k-i-k-o.com/projects/nike-talking-trash

Olympics webinar: olympics.com/athlete365/beat-the-heat

Player's Own Voice: cbc.ca/playersvoice/entry/i-worry-that-climate-change-is-crushing-athletic-limits

Reports

Goldblatt, David, and Rapid Transition Alliance. *Playing against the Clock: Global Sport, the Climate Emergency and the Case for Rapid Change.* playthegame.org/publications/playing-against-the-clock

Play It Forward: Innovating for the Next Generation: NHL Green Sustainability Report. nhl.com/community/nhl-green

Websites and Blogs

Balls 4 Eyeballs: balls4eyeballs.org

Climate Pledge Arena: climatepledgearena.com

EcoAthletes: ecoathletes.org

Ellis Spiezia: ellysium.co

Environmental Protection Agency: epa.gov

Forest Green Rovers: fgr.co.uk

Green Sports Alliance: greensportsalliance.org

Hylo Athletics: hyloathletics.com

Jadir Taekwondo Association (AJTKD): ajtkd.org

Loopt: loopt.org

MLB: mlb.com

NASCAR: nascar.com/impact

NHL: nhl.com/community/nhl-green

Nike Grind: nikegrind.com

On Running: on-running.com

One Tree Planted: playfortrees.org

Oracle Park: mlb.com/giants/ballpark

Players for the Planet: playersfortheplanet.org

Protect Our Winters: protectourwinters.org/pow-international

Sailors for Sustainability: sailorsforsustainability.nl

We Play Green: weplaygreen.com

WM Phoenix Open: wmphoenixopen.com/sustainability

ACKNOWLEDGMENTS

As always, putting together a book takes countless hours of research and fact-checking. Getting to work with or meet people who care so deeply about sports and the planet was inspiring, and I hope it "hits home" for readers too. I have so many people to thank for their help with this book. Whether they gave me information, interviews or photos, or hosted me in-person, I couldn't have written *In It to Win It* without them. In no particular order, I'd like to give the following people and organizations a big shout-out:

- The team at Oracle Park, including Chef T and Casey Baksa for the amazing tour in San Francisco
- Lee Spivak from Waste Management for an in-depth interview
- Ivar Smits and Floris van Hees, the Sailors for Sustainability, for calling me from somewhere on their adventure around the world!
- Chris Dickerson, Players for the Planet, for all the time he took to enthusiastically tell me about his organization's work
- Scott Welch from Loopt for the great interview about issues with sports apparel
- Kristen Fulmer and Lew Blaustein, EcoAthletes, for all their guidance and help connecting me with athletes and information from the very start of this process through to the end
- Ellis Spiezia for chatting with me about his passion
- Dr. Seth Wynes for his great research
- Dr. Matthew Cramer for sharing his expertise
- Amy Steel for an amazing personal interview about how climate change impacted her health
- Brianna Treat from Climate Pledge Arena for telling me all about their great work in Seattle
- Paula Brown from the Forest Green Rovers for giving me information about her organization
- Danilo Malafaia from AJTKD for sharing all the ways his organization is helping children in Brazil

And, of course, I have to thank my friends and family for visiting stadiums with me and giving me advice, information and links to articles and organizations. To Hilary, Kirstie and the team at Orca, thanks for helping me shape ideas into proposals and proposals into books, especially ones that matter. I will always be grateful for the opportunity to make a difference. I hope this book scores with readers!

INDEX

*Page numbers in **bold** indicate an image caption.*

ERIN SILVER is a children's author and freelance writer whose work has appeared in everything from *Good Housekeeping* to the *Washington Post*. She is the author of numerous books for children, including *Rush Hour: Navigating Our Global Traffic Jam* in the Orca Footprints series and *Good Food, Bad Waste: Let's Eat for the Planet* in the Orca Think series, as well as *What Kids Did: Stories of Kindness and Invention in the Time of COVID-19* and *Proud to Play: Canadian LGBTQ+ Athletes Who Made History*. Erin holds a master of fine arts in creative nonfiction from the University of King's College in Halifax, a postgraduate journalism degree from Toronto Metropolitan University and a bachelor of arts from the University of Toronto.

PUI YAN FONG is a Toronto-based illustrator. Originally from Hong Kong, she grew up in Toronto and studied illustration at Ringling College of Art and Design. She spends most of the day on her laptop, working on illustrations, reading or gaming. She is also a huge sports fan.